WHAT THE OTHER HALF DON'T KNOW

My Life as a transvestite escort (and how I became one)

Peter Edwards

authorHOUSE®

AuthorHouse™ UK Ltd.
500 Avebury Boulevard
Central Milton Keynes, MK9 2BE
www.authorhouse.co.uk
Phone: 08001974150

First published by AuthorHouse 3/11/2010

ISBN: 978-1-4490-9389-1 (sc)

This book is printed on acid-free paper.

I would like to thank and dedicate this book to the following people.

My three wives for they have each played a part in the creation of Susie, especially my last wife.

My son for teaching me how to use these electrical gadgets (computers) which have opened up a whole new life for me.

My friends Jenny and Cheryl who between them seem to be able to put up with me (especially my singing)

My 2 loving and faithful dogs who are always by my side with never ending love no matter how I am dressed or in whatever mood I may be in.

Most of all my departed father, not only for my very existence but also for setting such high standards for me to follow. Although my years with him were too few his impression on me has never waned. There is never an hour in my awakened days that I ever stop thinking about him with love and admiration even after 50 years. " Thanks Dad" I hope one day we will again be together (Then I bet some sparks will fly)

CONTENTS

Chapter 1. Going through with it   1

Chapter 2. How it all began   17

Chapter 3. Moving On   27

Chapter 4. Devastation   42

Chapter 5. Growing up   53

Chapter 6. Boy to man?   75

Chapter 7. In business   89

Chapter 8. Taking over   113

Chapter 9. The hangman   133

Chapter 10. Little bo peep   143

Chapter 11. The P.e. Politician   155

Chapter 12. The couple   169

Chapter 13. The boyfriend   180

Chapter 14. Taking the piss   193

Chapter 15. Twist in the tale   206

Chapter 16. Concluding thoughts   215

Chapter 1:
GOING THROUGH WITH IT

Ding-Dong as the doorbell rang, my heart was in my mouth, could I actually go through with it? How was I going to be able to open the door dressed as I was without being seen by the neighbours? As I stood there in my pinstriped suit with short skirt, white silky top with ruffles on the collar and cuffs, glossy seamed black stockings and black patent high-heeled shoes. All topped off with a blonde wig, heavy make-up, and lots of bling jewellery, oh and dowsed with a bottle full of cheap perfume, god I thought they will smell me before any one sees me. Never the less as I looked in the mirror by the front door, I thought to myself, that my ex wife hadn't done a bad job in creating Susie, this being the name she gave to her creation. I must admit I rather liked the idea of being called Susie when dressed, and as most of my clothes were of the tarty look I was soon given the nickname of Slapper Susie, which was I suppose very appropriate for my new solo career. Yes, I thought the client had asked for a smart tart secretary and that's what he has got, but how the hell am I going to open that bloody door dressed as I am. You see up to this point my ex wife had always opened the door, and as she was a naturally smart sexy women, none of the neighbours would think twice about seeing her looking like this, but now we are separated I have to do this on my own if I want to carry on with our little business which had been growing very nicely over the last 6 years or so. I am getting too old to carry on with my career as a builder, especially after 2 heart attacks and a mild stroke [from all of which I made a full recovery, thank the lord]. What with the weather and the hard manual labour, it was getting too much for me, so it made perfect sense to me to carry on with what we had started. It's a job that I can do and do well, so here I go deep breath and open that bloody door. As I opened the door I stood to one side to obscure my appearance from any prying eyes. "Come in darling" I said with a confident voice, and as if I were a commanding officer in the armed forces, he instantly did just that. I immediately closed the door behind him making sure it was securely locked, then turned to face him for the first time, he slowly looked me up and down and with a pleasant smile on his face said, "WOW you look fabulous". With that said my heart returned to its normal place, thank god he likes what he sees I thought. "Follow me through to the living room darling" I said and as I walked ahead of him clicking my heels on the wood block laid floor I could feel his eyes staring at me, and when we reached the living room, I turned round to face him once again, and sure enough his eyes were firmly fixed to my long shapely legs encased in glossy nylon, "take a seat darling, whilst I fix us both a drink". "Thank you Susie I will have a coffee 2 sugars please", came the very nervous reply, then I suddenly remembered that he was probably more nervous than I am, after all he is in a strange place, not knowing me, and in an environment completely new to him. This boosted my confidence no end. After making the coffee I sat in the living room opposite him in a chair that had been strategically placed before he arrived, ensuring that he had a good view of my legs as this is my best feature, but more importantly he could also see my lace top of my stockings. Sure enough as we were making small talk about the weather and his job as an officer in the army, his eyes were firmly affixed to my black, silky, stocking clad legs, and only raising his eyes for a second to answer my insignificant questions' but I did find that by talking to him about his life had a calming effect on his nerves, [and mine as well come to that]. As we sipped our coffee, and he was getting more relaxed, I noticed his eyes had become more in search of the rest of my body, so every now and then just to compensate I would cross my legs very slowly, ensuring that he got a good glimpse of my stocking tops, as by now my already short skirt had risen even more. Sure enough his eyes were immediately drawn back to my legs, I had to smile to myself, as my mind went straight back to one of those funny Kenny Everett sketches [all done in the best possible taste], and every now and then all he would say was "you have got a gorgeous pair of legs "."What about the rest of me then?" I would say "oh you really are very convincing and attractive" came his reply, now my confidence really was boosted and I was ready for anything. I now know how you girls feel when compliments are paid to you, [wonderful feeling], I now felt in complete control and acted accordingly. Then when the conversation had died, and in a moment's silence I looked at him with a cheeky but sexy smile on my face and asked, "well what sort of role play would you like darling? "He immediately lowered his eyes back to my legs and replied in a quiet voice, "you will probably think that I am weird when I tell you". My mind flashed back to all of those really way out weird customers my wife and I had done as a duo and thinking oh god what does this one want. Preparing myself for a shock and trying to keep in complete control, I calmly said " there is nothing that you can say will shock me darling, I have heard it all, so come on tell your little Susie all your fantasies". "Well" he said "I would like to be coming to you for an interview as an assistant to yourself, you being the lady boss of a successful business, and that you are a rather bossy bitch always getting your own way. I would also like you to humiliate me during the interview and always be talking down to me, in other words I want to feel inferior to you, yet at the same time need the job badly, you can sense that so you really put me through my paces, and get me to do all sorts of things to try to impress you." Well I thought that's an easy one to do, I am right at home doing that, I thought that it was going to be something much more difficult. "Right you wait here a minute whilst I go and prepare my office with a few props for our little game" I said," and when I am ready I will give you a shout, then after a couple of minutes knock my office door and wait for me to give you instructions to enter". "Alright mistress" he solemnly replied, as I stood up to leave the room I turned to him, pointed my finger at him and said " you had better be on your best behaviour and impress me or you will be punished". His eyes lit up like two headlights on a car, I knew then that he would be like putty in my hands. When I finally got to my office after leaving my officer with his tongue hanging out, I rearranged my two desks with one facing the other. My desk being the larger one with a nice swivel chair and his smaller one with a wooden kitchen chair [no comfort for him]. I placed a few insignificant papers on my desk and a few on his, a cheap ball point pen for him and a fountain pen for me along with a plastic ruler, then sat in a commanding position in my chair and waited for the knock on my door. After a couple of minutes came that feeble little knock on my door, very quiet I thought so I will make him wait and knock again until he can put a little more effort in his calling to draw my attention. KNOCK KNOCK that's better I thought, but I will still make him wait a little longer before giving him instructions to enter. After what could only be about two minutes, but must have seemed like a lifetime to him, I replied in a stern voice "ENTER". The door opened slowly and in he walked, I purposely kept my head down and made out that I was too busy writing something to take any notice of him, and was not prepared to acknowledge his presence until I was ready. He stood there in front of me head hung low waiting for my attention. "Yes what can I do for you?" I said with a stern but sexy voice. "Oh I have come for an interview for the vacant position of your personal secretary". "You're late" I said "where have you been, and what is your excuse for your bad timekeeping?"

"Sorry miss but I had to go to the gents, I think it must be nerves or something like that."

" Firstly you do not call me miss, to you its either madam or mistress, do I make myself clear?" " Yes mistress" was his sombre reply. "Good that's that fact established, now did you wash your hands?" I asked.

"Yes mistress" " let me see" I instructed. He slowly held out his soft hands, which I don't think had ever done a days hard graft in their lives. "Turn them over, now go and wash them again, and after you have done that make me a cup of coffee and bring it to me. You may have a glass of water." "Yes mistress " came the excited reply. Upon his return as he placed my coffee on my desk as he did he accidentally dropped some coffee on my shoes, now if he did this on purpose or not I do not know, but it was the perfect opportunity for me to reprimand him for his misdemeanour. "Look what you have done to my new shoes," I said "I'm sorry mistress" was his pathetic reply. "Get that duster from my shelf and get down and clean them immediately you useless article." As quick as a flash he grabbed the duster and then fell to his knees at my feet. "Lick that coffee off first then polish my shoes." "Yes mistress I will

I am so so sorry." "You will be in a minute", I said, "I cannot let that go unpunished." I could see the expression on his face beaming with excitement. I knew then that I had him exactly where I wanted him, and that I could end this little charade whenever I wished to. That's always the battle in this game, knowing how far you can take them before they climax and then working backwards, to fill in their time, making sure that they enjoy every little thing that you do to them. He licked my shoes over and over again, then rubbed them gently with the duster until they gleamed once again like patent shoes should do. "Now get up and stand before me" I commanded. "Yes mistress" he replied, and as he got up I could quite clearly see his excitement forcing a large bulge in the front of his trousers. " I must now punish you for your lack of ability in serving me with drinks, that will be one of your chores, amongst many others. I sometimes work on late in the evenings and as a result you will of course work with me irrespective of time, is that understood?" "Yes mistress" he squeaked. "Right, now for your punishment, you will lower your trousers and lay over my desk placing your nose in a circle of chalk strategically placed on my desk, and if your nose leaves that circle whilst I administer the punishment, I will double the amount of strokes from six to twelve, is that clear?" "Oh yes mistress" came the excited reply, as he fumbled with his belt and zip of his trousers I looked closely at him and could see the enjoyment in his face, being in a situation that I am sure that he has never in his adult life been in before. As he stood there before me with his very stiff erection and his trousers around his ankles, I placed one hand on the back of his neck and forced him over my desk, I then took my plastic ruler and gave him six of the best, not that hard at all, for most of the subs it's the thought, not the action that gives them the thrill, so you must be careful not to go over the top and kill the game stone dead, I made him count out loud every stroke and thank me after each one, this he did, and true to form on the sixth one he lifted his nose out of the circle, that was a sign that he wanted more , so he got them. After the punishment I made him once again stand before me, with all of his glory on show, so with his glass of water poured cold water over his manhood, "punishment to fit the crime" I exclaimed. "Yes mistress" he said with a shaky voice, even with cold water being poured over his pride, it still stood to attention. By now he was really into his role as my sub secretary, so it was time to give him more duties. "Sit at your desk!" I exclaimed and as he struggled to walk with his trousers around his ankles, he went to bend down to pick them up. "I didn't give you permission to pull your trousers up did I?" "No mistress" he murmured. "Well then leave them there, no better still take them off all together, and those stupid colourful boxer shorts, and let me see just how much of a man you really are, or not whatever the case may be." How I didn't laugh whilst watching him trying to remove his clothes with his shoes still on I shall never know. Eventually he removed his shoes enabling him to remove all that I had asked for, and there he stood before me naked from the waist down with all on display. Although he was about average in his manhood size, I naturally commented on its saying, "what on earth do you think you can achieve with that little thing." "I don't know mistress" was his feeble reply and just to add insult to injury I took my plastic ruler and placed it along side of his erect penis making sure that I didn't measure it correctly by keeping the ruler up from the base, and sure enough it would only measure about 4inches, [in reality it was about normal as I said roughly 5-6 inches]. "There" I said " see only 4 inches what good is that thing to any normal woman, are you married? " yes mistress" he replied. "Well I pity your poor wife, she must be very frustrated." " I don't know mistress" he spoke now in a very low voice and his head lowered. Whilst I had the ruler in my hand I decided to gently smack his hard shaft with it, causing it to spring back to its erect position after every smack, this amused me and made me laugh a girlish giggle, all of which turned him on even more by letting out hushed pleasurable moans. "Go and sit at your desk" I commanded, "and take down in your best handwriting a letter which I will dictate to you." As he sat on his hard chair behind his small desk, I purposely sat on his desk top close to him, then crossing my legs right in front of his face very slowly, making sure that he could see all of my stocking tops. Although he had a pen in his hand he was certainly not looking at his writing paper, with that I picked up an old letter I had at hand and started to read from it for him to copy. As I read out long sentences I would purposely talk quickly ensuring that he couldn't keep up, whilst at the same time kept fidgeting my legs until they were touching his naked thighs. The feel of that silky nylon against his bare skin was too much for him to concentrate any longer, and with his spare hand started to masturbate himself. "WHAT on earth do you think you are doing?" I sternly said. "I am so sorry mistress" he replied." Let me look at your standard of writing, its simply appalling look at it." His head lowered in pitiful shame, "yes mistress I am so worked up looking at your gorgeous legs that I just can't stop myself." I knew then that we had reached the point of no return and he just had to be relieved, after all time is time and he was very near his quota. "Well I think that you had better get around to my desk and lay on the floor by my feet as I need a foot rest whilst I finish off this letter which must be completed by lunchtime." "Yes mistress" came his reply with a touch of relief in his voice." Lay under my desk and place your hands by your side on your back and straight", this he did immediately. I then sat on my swivel chair and spun it around so that I was directly over him, placed one foot on his chest making sure that the heel made an impression on him [to which he gave a pleasurable moan] then with the other foot placed it firmly on his manhood making sure that the heel was in his scrotum and the sole firmly against his stiff manhood, now he really did moan. With just gentle movements at first I slid my foot up and down his throbbing penis, his whole body was shaking with excitement, and his moans were getting louder, I knew he wasn't far of climaxing so I kicked off my shoe and with my nylon clad foot against his almost bursting shaft, brought him to a satisfactory climax, to which he almost screamed with delight. As he lay there with a smile on his face from ear to ear, eyes closed, and contented breaths, I looked down on him and thought if they are all as easy as this I shall be more than happy. "Well darling I bet you would like a nice shower now wouldn't you?" "Oh yes please Susie"[by now the mistress bit was dropped]." Let me show you where the shower is and I will make us both a nice cup of coffee." "? That would be lovely," he said. When he came back downstairs from his shower re dressed in his smart suit we sat down together drank our coffee and reminisced over his fantasy and how much he had really enjoyed himself, he told me that he was very high up in the forces [a ranking that I am not going to divulge for obvious reasons] and that all of his military life he has given commands and people jumped to his every word, but deep down he wanted the shoe on the other foot for once. "Oh I said did I use the wrong foot?" He laughed then looked at me and said, "you certainly didn't Susie." He then paid me my fee, with a little bonus, kissed me on the cheek, and said, "I will definitely be back!" True to his word has paid me several visits, each one similar to the first with slight variations. After he had said his goodbyes and left, I sat on my sofa with another drink and thought to myself what a gentleman he was, how I wish they could all be like him, just a simple mild domination, where as a lot of them are really into heavy complicated domination, which believe you me is very taxing on the brain to successfully. Then I began to wonder just how my life had developed to bring me to where I am now with all of its sinister twists.

Peter Edwards

Chapter 2
HOW IT ALL BEGAN

Unbeknown to me at the time but life's lessons on preparation to face the outside world came early with stark differences and harsh reality.

I was born in a luxury 3 bedroom detached house recently built by my Father a master builder with a large construction company. He was the first builder to build new houses in our area and in those early days just after the Second World War was licensed to do so but unfortunately he was not a healthy man. Although he always looked a picture of health with his dark tan he had suffered with rheumatic fever as a child leaving him with heart problems resulting in him spending time in hospital a victim of frequent heart attacks and a stroke. Little did I know that I too would experience the same in later life.

As any person in business will know the early days require you to be there leading from the front, taking control and organising but due to his forced absence through time spent in hospital and at home convalescing the company was forced into liquidation.

Gone was the luxury detached house replaced by an end of terrace slum property bought by my mother for the princely sum of £80 still cheap even in those post war years. Where once I lived in relative comfort and a garden to play in I now was faced with no bathroom or running hot water, a WC in a cupboard in my parents bedroom and our only water from a stand pipe in the rickety kitchenette lashed up against the back wall of the house. The street now became my playground.

From being driven around in my fathers Jaguar I was reduced to sitting on the crossbar of a pushbike which had now become the family's only means of transport. Primarily used to take my father to work as a subcontract bricklayer. I would travel with him on holidays and weekends on that crossbar to his place of work as a labourer to supplement his meagre income.

These are amongst my earliest memories as I loved going off to work with my Dad but also remember losing the feeling in my legs as a result of tucking them up out of the way to allow him to steer but to me a small price to pay for being in his company.

During the first fourteen years of my life I experienced extreme highs and lows as my Dad rose to the height of his profession with the trappings of being a successful businessman to the depths of bankruptcy twice over another parallel which would occur to me in my later life worshipped and looked up to my Dad and learnt from him determination as he never stopped working hard or trying to improve his lot even up to the day he died just before my fifteenth birthday just as he was rising to the top for the third time.

Whilst I idolised him I often tried my father's patience beyond belief as I was at times a really naughty boy. I can honestly say I deserved every thrashing he ever gave me. Poor old Dad tried everything with me from locking me in the dark cellar, to talking to me on a man to man basis and finally a bloody good hiding which always seemed to work the best. Little did I know that in later life I could put these experiences to a profitable use!

Looking back I am glad of his strict approach as it prepared me for what I was to face in my early adult life.

Although being a boisterous child I had a hidden side, which would soon manifest itself. I have heard from many family members and my Mothers own lips that she had always wanted a little girl as her second child already having a three and a half year old son my one and only brother, but she had me instead, little did she know that deep within me was the daughter she always wanted.

Up until the age of three she kept my blonde hair long and curly and as a result those who didn't know often mistook me for a girl. Whether my Mother encouraged this or not I have no knowledge but what I do know is that the bond between my mother and I was different to the one she shared with my elder brother who up to the time of publishing this book has had no knowledge of my feminine side.

I can remember from the age of six I would love to dress in my mother's stockings and shoes and whatever other of her clothes I could get hold of. Not too out of the ordinary you might think and all seemingly quite innocent for that tender age. Even in those early days stockings seemed to fascinate I and I can still vividly remember that lovely silky feeling when they first touched my naked smooth skin.

In those years it was customary for children to be sent to bed early whether you were tired or not and I was no different being put to bed at 7.30 p.m. In the long summers we had then it would still be daylight at that time and I would remember lying in bed for what seemed to be hours before falling asleep thinking even at that age how ridiculous it was to go to bed in bright sunlight.

I t was on one such night having been put to bed a little earlier as my parents were entertaining some friends that I discovered the hidden delights of a chest of drawers that occupied the corner of my room. As a result of moving to our smaller house following the collapse of my dads business there was not enough space in my parents bedroom to house all my mothers clothes and this chest became the overspill for some of her things-namely stockings and underwear- very handy.

Being wide awake and full of energy the chest of drawers became a centre of attention and I began to wonder what lay within. So boys being boys I decided to investigate. When I opened the drawers to my delight I found layers of silky stockings and lacy fabrics the feel of which sent shivers of excitement through me which I had not experienced before.

As I continued to rummage through the drawers I came across stockings, knickers, bras, slips and all sorts of garments new to me.

Something inside of me awakened for the first time and I was overcome with the desire to put these wonderful feeling garments on. Within minutes I had peeled off my pyjamas and now stood there dressed in knickers and stockings I walked around the room delighting in how I felt admiring myself in the mirror of the wardrobe door. At this point I remembered that there were further clothes and shoes of my mothers inside and so I opened the door and put on a fox fur stole which was hanging there my eyes were now drawn to the shoes neatly stored at the bottom of the wardrobe. I picked out a pair of high heels and slipped my feet into them. They were like barges on my impish feet but I didn't care as I felt that I had woken an exciting side of me I did not know existed. Whilst admiring the new me in the mirror I realised the look was incomplete when I pictured my mother dressed this way and remembered a dish of makeup on top of the chest of drawers along with some items of jewellery that had been left there. So I turned and stumbled in my new footwear back to the chest of drawers. Once there I put on some powder lipstick and perfume and adorned myself with the jewellery. What a sight I must have looked at six years of age I had no clue of what make up to put on where or how much of it to use.

Whether it was the noise of the heels clunking across the lino of the bedroom floor I don't know but to my astonishment the bedroom door opened and there stood my tall dark handsome father. Looking like a cross between

Robert Mitchum and James Garner he was often mistaken for a film star with an excellent physique obtained from his days as a Royal Marine where he employed his muscular frame as a heavy weight boxer representing the corps.

At this point I was quaking in my oversize shoes anticipating one of his typical violent punishments for my usual boisterous misdemeanours. I can still remember the embarrassment I felt as the blood rushed to my face making me blush redder than the rouge I had applied to my cheeks. But to my surprise the silence was deafening he just picked me up in his strong arms and carried me downstairs to the living room. As we got to the foot of the stairs I could hear the conversation between my mother and my parent's friends but as we entered the room a deathly hush descended.

In the silence my Dad placed me in the middle of the floor between my mother and their quests who were old friends and known to me as "Uncle Bob and Auntie Hilda".

I sat there embarrassed and in silence as I was taught as little boys are seen and never heard and never speak until you are spoken too whilst at the same time still fearing my expected thrashing.

After what seemed like hours to me but in reality was probably only a few minutes the conversation resumed and my presence ignored.

Within a short period I began to fall asleep, at which point my father picked me up and carried me back to my room again with nothing being said. He put me into bed dressed in all my finery minus the shoes.

Nothing was ever mentioned by my father about that fateful event and neither by my mother and I was certainly never going to bring it up.

After that little episode my cross dressing moments were limited to only when the house would be empty or when it was really safe to do so as I did not want a repeat of that experience again. To this day the reactions of my parents to that event still baffle me.

Chapter 3
MOVING ON

By the time I was eight years old my father was in the process of rebuilding his business and talk was afoot of moving to a better house. Away from the slum property we occupied in the cold windy north east to Bournemouth a place where as a family we had previously spent two summer holidays where we had fallen in love with the beautiful beaches, tree lined avenues and where the sun always seemed to shine.

My father who not only built but also designed beautiful detached houses were years ahead of the rest of the market and as Bournemouth was a rich place it seemed the obvious choice for his business to flourish.

And as for my mother, brother and I the choice between living in the cold miserable Northeast or the sun drenched south coast well; there was just no competition.

The big move came when I was nine years old and my father who wasn't a man to do things by half rented a large six bed roomed detached house with massive gardens and orchard with a one hundred yard gravelled drive for us to live in until his business was established and was in a position to build our own house. A contrast to the two bed roomed slum we left under the ball of the demolition hammer.

What an exciting adventurous time that was in my life. As both of my parents were involved with the running of the business my brother and I had to learn to fend for ourselves as my mother and father would be off buying land or at meetings leaving us to get ourselves to school or make our own meals. This also left me to my own devices and yes you guessed it opportunity to dress in this massive house with three bathrooms and locks on the doors!!!!!!

Fortunately for me my young attractive mother was very fashion conscious and with our regained wealth was busy expanding her wardrobe. It was now that I started to take more notice of ladies fashion especially as the shortages of the post war years were now past and heels were getting higher and thinner, dresses and skirts more revealing and in particular stockings more readily available and in a wider range of colours and styles. With seams, in American Tan, black, dark brown and WOW fishnet too! A huge difference to the gravy browning and eyebrow pencil seamed legs I had been used too!

As Bournemouth is a very large town with lots of pretty ladies every where you seem to look and all seemingly very fashionable keeping up with the latest styles. My own mother was no exception to doing the same, she even used to buy those women's mags showing off those latest fashions, which I would adoringly gaze at whilst safely locked in one of the bathrooms and living in my own fantasy world. Sometimes for hours but at the same time taking close attention of all those wonderful new styles being shown off by absolutely gorgeous models. Whenever I could get the chance to have some private moments in an empty house [which wasn't that often] I would visit my mothers bedroom to explore the wonders in her wardrobe and emulate those pretty girls from those magazines to the best of my ability. The strangest thing is that at the same time all this was going on with my feminine side of life, my boyish ways were getting more boisterous I was always getting into trouble of some kind or another fighting at school, purposely failing to obey school rules, being given lines for doing so and asking for the cane instead, after which I would tell the teacher who had just administered the punishment: that didn't hurt: even though believe you me it bloody well did, but I would not let them know that. I was even hauled up in front of the headmaster who had asked for my father also to be present and then told " boy you hold the record for having your name in the punishment book more than any other boy in the history of this school". Not one of my proudest moments I have never seen my fathers face go so red with fury, needless to say that when things calmed down a bit they both talked to me in a civilised way about changing my ways, then turned round and made me vice form captain, very appropriate I thought. Any way it seemed to do the trick I pulled my socks up and started to get better annual exam results as well as representing the school in swimming, football, athletics, and yes you guessed it boxing. So you see the gap was definitely getting wider within me my two sides was like chalk and cheese, a fact that I was very much aware of and indeed was to wrestle with in the many years that lay ahead. By the time I had reached 11 years old I found myself joining the local ice skating ring along with a school pal. Where most Saturday afternoons were spent falling down getting soaked on the wet ice, getting cut and bruised, and generally making bloody fools of ourselves until we had mastered the finer arts of skating, if you can call it that. More important than that the ice rink was full of pretty females most of which were dressed in those tiny little skirts which flared out and new to me at that time tights, glossy ones, sparkly ones, but above all lots and lots of leg on display. I fell madly in love every Saturday afternoon with a different girl, especially with the ones that showed the most glossy nylon covered legs. I still don't know whether it was the girl or her tights I had fallen for. How I wanted a pair of those tights for myself to feel against my own skin, however looking back at this time of my life its apparent to me that this must have been around the time when testosterone was rising and testicles were dropping. By the time I was approaching 12, my fathers business was going well he was by now building some 6 houses per year and I wanted to be part of it. As I always loved working with my father, I asked if I could help out at week-ends and school holidays and dear old dad duly obliged by informing his works foreman that I was to start work in the coming school summer holidays and that I was not to be treated any different to any one else. Although he was a strict man he was also a very kind and fair man he could not give to one without the other which meant as kids my brother and I each got the same, so when it was his birthday I also got a present and visa versa. I still to this day worship the ground he ever walked on and I am sure I speak for my brother as well. So off to work I went and can honestly say that I enjoyed every second of it. I just couldn't wait until I left school to work for my hero dad, learn a trade and make him proud of me. All of this activity left me very little time to pursuit my ice skating beauties, or to indulge in my private dressing escapades, well after all I am working now learning to lay bricks, its time to grow out of that phase now, or so I thought. But by the time the darker autumn evenings were upon us I started to yearn for that touch of femininity again. It's strange but every time those feelings returned the intensity grew stronger, which in turn gave me cause for concern as it seemed to me that I was becoming two separate people each with a strengthening will to grow. To compensate for my anxiety I did the only thing I thought was best and decided to follow my more manly instincts and get out on Saturday afternoons with some of my school pals and chase the girls. I took to this like a duck to water, overcoming my shyness I plucked up courage and asked a girl who went to the all girls school next to my school [very convenient] to the pictures and to my pleasant surprise she accepted. With the extra pocket money I received from my holiday work I was able to treat her. I was the proper little gentleman and dutifully escorted her safely back to her house after the film, calling into the new wimpy bar en route. I don't know wither she sang my praises at her school or not, but I couldn't go wrong after that, so every Saturday afternoon was spent at the pictures, at the ice rink, or in a wimpy bar.

Its funny but all the girls I seemed to be attracted too, where the ones who wore stockings, as not all of the girls approaching their teens could probably afford them. I was a confirmed leg man even those early days. I can even remember clearly on one occasion asking a girl to dress up smartly and put a new pair of stockings on for the forthcoming date, with a cheeky smile on my face, and surprise surprise she did just that. Can you imagine saying that to today's modern girl I think it would be more than a cheeky smile you would have on your face! Nevertheless I can quite honestly say that I really enjoyed myself stroking all those lovely nylon clad legs in the back seat of the local cinema, for stroking was as far as I was able to get in those days. Indeed I don't think I knew then what else there was to do, but just to feel that silky material seemed to satisfy Peter, but awaken my feminine side beyond belief. Then out of the blue my father was taken seriously ill again with 2 further heart attacks and back into hospital he went. No doubt caused through the stress of his demanding business as another one of those troughs in the ups and downs of the unstable financial market occurred resulting in being left with expensive properties unsold and banks calling in their loans. Fortunately a small blessing for my father was the fact that his company was a limited company, but like all self made firms he did have to put up personnel assurances. As a consequence the lovely new house that my father had built for us and we were now occupying had to be sold along with all the other assets. This included the latest Jaguar car, which was replaced by a little old van my mother had bought out of her meagre savings for £150. Here we go again I thought, still its better than that pushbikes crossbar. So my father went back on the tools and secured a sizeable contract to build 80 houses on a labour only basis in a small town in Somerset about 50miles from Bournemouth where life seemed positively middle aged compared to the faster pace of life in Bournemouth. There were though certain advantages to be taken into consideration; mainly the new school I was about to attend for my last 18 months of education was a mixed school, umm! After being used to boys only this was quite a novelty, and some of these little beauties with their strange

Somerset accents were not backwards in coming forwards [if you know what I mean]. This new estate my father was about to build was right next to the school I was attending and my mother being a shrewd business person in her own rights had not only saved enough money for the van but enough also for a deposit on one of the new houses my father was building. So all in all not far to walk to school, able to work with my dad on the tools as we were living on the job, and lots of new girlfriends, who were equally amused with my accent as I was with theirs. MY older brother had been working with dad for about three and a half years had by now passed his driving test enabling him to take some of the burden off dad's shoulders. He was also my father's eyes and ears when dad wasn't around, a bit like a foreman. As the main brickwork sub-contractor he obviously couldn't do all the brickwork with just my brother so he employed about 20 men consisting of mainly bricklayers and hood carriers [one of which I was to become] then split them into two gangs one of which my brother looked after. So the new business was far less stressful for dads health, and as I said right on our doorstep so I didn't have far to go when leaving school to pick my hod up and load out the scaffold ahead of the following gang of brickies to give them a start. I loved every second of this time in my life working with my dad and counting down the days to leaving school when I could be full time. I was seldom put to work with my brother on whatever gang he was looking after as we fought like cat and dog. Poor old dad was forever trying to split us up at home so he certainly didn't want disharmony at work he could never understand why as brothers we argued so much, and dad would often say to me "why do you fight so much with your brother? You know he is bigger and stronger than you and he is going to beat you every time". "Perhaps so dad, but one day he wont", I would reply. Thank god we grew out of that stage of our lives before one of us got killed. Although it was to be quite a few years before we did, even so we were always there for each other when support was needed. We even joined a local pop group together, as I had played the drums in the school orchestra, and my brother had played guitar in a skiffle band whilst in Bournemouth, it was about the only time we would speak to each other in a civil manner. We would practise most nights of the week, and after about 4 weeks we were bearable and you could just about recognise whatever tune we were trying to play. My father who was curious with us as brothers going out together, coming home later in the evening together and me not covered in blood, came along one evening to see for himself just what this new found venture was that helped us to bond as brothers. Well we must have surprised dad because the very next day when I got home from school to my splendid surprise there in front of me was a full set of Premier drums, which he had been and bought for me that same day, as I had been playing on a borrowed set for the last 4 weeks and the owner wanted them back. As I have previously mentioned dad was a very fair man and so as not to show favouritism he also bought my brother a new bass guitar. What a hero where he got the money from god knows, but he got it. That very evening when we went to practise with our new instruments we felt like pop stars, [didn't make us sound any better but felt like it]. The two other boys, who played in the band with us, looked on with envy in their eyes, which my father noticed. In a flash he said "come on boys I want you to sit down and write me a list of equipment that you two need and I will get it for you, and when you make your first million you can pay me back". There are no words to explain the look of joy on there faces as they both came from broken backgrounds where money was scarce, and I for one was so proud to have such a father. With a little more practice we were soon good enough to go out and perform in front of the local general public in a village hall next to the local pub. In those days there were no discos just raw live bands, and we seemed to go down well especially when playing 'lets twist again like we did last summer'. I lost count how many times we played that number on that eventful evening but they loved it, and so did my parents who attended that dance along with most of my dads workforce for our first gig. Now whether it was the fact that dad had too much to drink or not I don't know but he even got up with my mother and actually danced the twist, the first time I had ever seen them dance. He looked so proud to see his sons entertaining around a hundred and fifty people all dancing and screaming encore every time we finished a number to rapturous applause. His pride was only matched by my own seeing my dad dancing to my beat; I felt 10 foot tall.

We progressed from that meagre village hall to perform in greater venues and my parents would come along to witness that progression as often as they could. More importantly to me on a feminine side, was the fact that I was able to see at first hand all of those stocking tops and stilettos as they spun around to my beat. I mean I was fourteen and these girls were as old as 20, women to my eyes. How I would flirt with them and try to chat them up, but I was only fourteen and they just thought I was cute. Little did they know that whilst staring at them with a cheeky smile, I was studying their clothes and make up wishing I could wear some of it. With all of this activity going on hod carrying, drumming etc there was very little time for my dressing escapades, but more importantly I could feel I was becoming a man, and certainly experienced that feeling with talk between my father and I becoming more and more man to man rather than man to boy, wonderful years for me.

Chapter 4
DEVASTATION

All was going well right up to the day I was to leave school, when at last I was going to work alongside my master craftsman hero dad, and to celebrate the coming event we were going to have a holiday in Switzerland. Dads business was on the up once more and there was even talk of him purchasing a small plot of land to build a bungalow on spec and mix in this new development project with his flourishing sub contract work. About one week before we were due to depart to foreign parts my dad who had been complaining of feeling ill after eating during the last couple of months, took a trip to the local doctors to get something a little stronger than previously prescribed for the forthcoming holiday. Whilst visiting the surgery the doctor gave him a good check over, taking into account his long history of heart problems, where upon he found that dads thrombosis in his legs was serious enough to admit him to hospital in Yeovil immediately. This was on the very day that I had just finished school it being the last day of term. The shock of this news as I ran into the living room, feeling elated from leaving school and that after the holiday I would be working full time with dad, hit me like a hammer, it seemed that the earth had just stopped spinning. "Don't worry dad, " I said "you have been there before and come back you will do it again". Despite this the shroud of gloom was well and truly over our house once again. My mother had even telephoned the holiday company to cancel the forthcoming trip, a bit drastic I thought, after all during my short life I had seen my father go to hospital several times with what I thought far more serious illnesses than thrombosis. However mother did cancel the holiday resulting in them loosing the already paid deposit as in those days holiday insurance was not like it is today, however looking back a small price to pay. Whilst in hospital my father was still complaining of his stomach pains after eating, so the hospital doctors said that he must have a stomach ulcer, and that they would on the following give him an exploratory operation to find the offending cause and remove it. We visited the hospital that evening to see dad when he came round from the anaesthetic, only to be ushered into a private consulting room. Then the consultant dropped his bombshell. " I am sorry to inform you, but we have found that your husband has got rapid cancer throughout his stomach and major organs, and he has only got seven days to live at the most". We stood there in a silence only to be broken by my mothers sobbing shortly followed by my brother and I doing the same. "You must not tell him what you now know. He is to be told that the operation was a success and that he is on the road to recovery, for if he knew the truth being so young at 41, and having such a young family shortly to be left without the kingpin of the household, would be too much for him to accept." I think that was one of the hardest things I have ever had to do, face my father at his bedside and talk to him about all the things we were going to do in the future together, yet all the time knowing he was very shortly going to die, and right up to the end he never knew the truth. I had never lied to my father in my life, as one of his pet hates was a liar, he even had one of his notorious sayings for that." I cant stand liars;" he would say "at least with a thief you can cut his hands off, but a liar will always be untrusted" so for me to now blatantly lie to him was foreign to my nature. I often had the feeling that he had an inkling of the truth, as he would try to trick me in our various conversations, as he also did with the rest of my family, but none of us ever succumbed to his trickery. As he thought that he was by now convalescing from his operation he asked if he could go home to get better as he had a huge dislike for hospitals. My brave mother discussed this task with the hospital doctors and they said that it could be done, and to keep up the charade we would have to go through with his request. They arranged to provide us with a permanent nurse to stay with us up to the end, he was told she was going to stay with us to administer his much needed medicines for his speedy recovery. Not only did he want to be allowed home, he also requested that he should go back to his home town in Lincolnshire where all our remaining family members still lived and finish his convalescing off in my aunts house. This was a very difficult task to accomplish, as special arrangements had to be made with British Rail [as it was then] for a special compartment to be provided on both the Yeovil to London train and the London to Lincolnshire train. With ambulances laid on in London for the journey across the city from one station to another, as well as ambulances in Lincolnshire the journey was successfully completed by my brave mother and hospital staff including the assigned nurse. All of this was done inside three days and I was to stay with my cousin some 16 miles away from my father's bedside, with the understanding that my cousin would take me to see dad every evening. The reason I stayed with my cousin was because my aunt's house was a small one and with most of my family and a live in nurse staying there, it was full. He lived exactly 7 days after his operation, and I am convinced that the only way that the doctors could be so accurate was because they knew how much pain killing drugs could be administered before his by now feeble body would close down. Even though I was 16 miles away when my father died, I knew the instant he took his last breath, something just came over me, I remember it as if it were yesterday. I was in my cousin's garden exercising his dog, when for no reason I looked up into the blue sky and said to myself dads just died. With that I walked up to my cousin's kitchen and said " you don't have to tell me but I think my dads just this second died." Before he could reply to my solemn statement the telephone rang, and still looking astonished by my recent statement my cousin answered the phone. The look on his face turned from astonishment to bewilderment as he received verbal confirmation of my fathers death, and without saying a word, replaced the receiver, walked over toward me and put his arms around me and hugged me as I let out the tears within me. After the main tears and in between my gulps of breath I asked him to drive me over to my aunt's [his mothers] house to be with my immediate family. With that said we walked to his car to take the 16mile journey, it seemed like 116 miles with every cat's eye passing in slow motion. When we arrived I went straight to my mother and brother who like me were still in floods of tears and tried to comfort each others sorrows as best we could, even though we knew the outcome some 7 days earlier it did still not soften the final blow. As word spread throughout the rest of the family members they each came in turn to pay their respects on that mournful night. As they arrived they each in turn walked into the front room where my father's corpse lay to say their final good bye. I repeatedly asked my mother for that same request, but was denied, being told that I was too young to see a dead person, and that if I did I would have nightmares over it for years to come. But I refused to accept that statement, saying "but that's not a dead person that's my dad and he would never hurt or frighten me in any way." Eventually I asked my understanding cousin who was not much younger than my mother if he would speak to my mother and let me see my dad. This he did and speaking in my defence said "let the boy see his father he is old enough to judge for himself" and with that said she granted me permission to see my dad. My cousin asked me if I wanted him to come with me, I replied " no I want to be on my own." I will always be indebted to my cousin for his assistance, and after seeing my father laid to rest with a look of peace on his face, came to terms with small comfort towards his death. After the funeral some 3 days later my mother brother and I decided that we had to go back to our home in Somerset and that my brother was to sack all of dads employees to close down his firm. At 18 my brother wasn't old enough to take over and I certainly wasn't so the closure decision was made. The journey back to Somerset was accompanied by my cousin, who also stayed with us for a few days whilst we formed some sort of direction as to where we were going. My mother was going to get a job in a ladies clothes shop, my brother was going to get some sub-contract brickwork [on a small scale] and I was to find a job with another builder, to finish off what my father had already started by learning my trade as a bricklayer. Ironic I thought to myself, all I ever wanted to do was to work for my father, and the day I left school to do so, he died I felt so cheated, and still do to this very day. I have never been a very religious person and with those recent events never likely to be. So I approached a fairly local builder who was building the new police station in our hometown in Somerset. He had known my father, mostly for what my dad had built, and from word of mouth throughout the small town in which we lived, and on the strength of that and what I had told him throughout my short interview secured a job as an improver bricklayer. Because of the knowledge I had already acquired in my short life he thought it best that I go straight as an improver, same wages as an apprentice 2 pounds 10 shillings per week [that's £2 50 in modern money]. The only problem was I could not get insurance cards until I was 15, in some 6 weeks time. I was told to keep this fact quiet and if any official looking bod [his words] came on site make yourself scarce, as he was breaking the law and I was not covered on his insurance. "Christ" I thought and we are building a bloody cop shop, that's a good start to my new career, still dad would have had the same problem so best get on with it. I used to get to work half an hour before any one else to get the mixer going and get the mortar boards loaded ready for an eight o clock start for every one else. I was in my element now, and soon learnt how to lay bricks as good as the next man, "not as fast but as good, speed will come with experience" Don my new boss would say and it did. Don or as his nickname was Donkey Don for obvious reasons you will shortly find out, was a real joker and I had to accept the fact that as the new boy I was going to be the brunt of many a prank, and I was. I soon learnt to give back as good as I got, which resulted in being less and less of the brunt. I remember well on one day in particular when it was very hot, Don and I were putting the large water storage tanks in the roof attic before the floor boards and plasterboard were fixed, because of the heat Don had told me to take 2 milk bottles full of water up with us to drink as we were likely to be up there for some time, this I did. Whilst we were up there a company rep walked in on the ground floor directly below us, shouting out his name, looking all around but not upwards, and as quick as a flash Don unzipped his fly took out his enormous penis with one hand, and with the other hand poured water on the unsuspected victim, where upon the rep looked up to see Don shaking this enormous penis saying "sorry mate I did not see you there." He ran out of the building wiping his neck never to return, and I nearly fell off the joists with laughter. Hence Donkey Don.

Chapter 5
GROWING UP

By the time winter was approaching the work on the new police station was nearing completion. The next project that Don was due to start was about 15 miles away from my hometown, which meant that I would have to rely on public transport. With the wages that I was receiving it was just not going to be viable, so I had to look for another job closer to home. As it happened the contract that my father was working on when he unfortunately died was not quite complete and so another sub contractor had been appointed to finish it. Living on the estate it seemed the obvious place to seek employment; I got the job and even managed to get a slight increase in wages. Up to 4 pounds per week and no travelling expenses, but with now having insurance cards deductions had to be made, so all in all just slightly better off, still better than nothing. The group was going stronger than ever now and as a result we were getting paid good money for our gigs, averaging about £20 per gig less petrol money plus the payments on the van we had purchased, split the rest 4 ways and every bit helped. I think that by keeping in the band after dads death helped my brother and I to get on with life and share our new found responsibilities as the only men in the house. Even though we as brothers still fought like cat and dog, as true professionals masked our arguments whilst on stage. Our progression with the band had lead us to the point where most weeks we would be performing at least five nights per week. Often playing on the same bill as some of the top groups at that time. , Ricky Valance who had the hit ' tell Laura I love her', Brian Poole and the Tremeloes, Dave Dee, Dozy, Beaky, Mick and Titch, to name just a few. The women followers that came with those big names absolutely blew my mind, and on occasions when we got the time had some memorable moments of joy with some of those girls, I suppose they would be called groupies by today's standards.

Never the less with all this work and driving all over England playing in the band, it left little time for any other activities, especially of the dressing kind, even though the desire was stronger than ever. As hard as I would try to suppress those desires they would not go away, and each time they reappeared, it was with more intensity, especially as my mother who was by now working full time in the fashionable ladies clothes shop was bringing home some of the latest fashions for herself at cost [perks of the job]. I would admire these at a safe distance, and wish that I could try them on. Unfortunately I had grown somewhat since those earlier days and with my physical job I was getting quite muscular, whilst my mother was very very slim weighing only about 7 stone a size 6 to 8, so I think something would have given, and blown my secret. Strangely enough since the death of my father, my relationship with my mother was starting to deteriorate and we didn't seem to have a lot in common, I was seeing my mother in a much different light, and in the absence of my father [the king pin] we were definitely drifting apart. I remember during the hard winter of 1963- 1964 having quite a few arguments with both my mother and my brother. Whilst those two were getting on fine, I seemed to be the odd one out, as my views on life in general were completely different to theirs, and as a result found myself getting more and more ignored. During the summer of 1964 my brother was having an affair with the married lady literally from next door. Unfortunately all at the same time as I was dating her daughter, who incidentally I had fallen madly in love with and she in return. This was the girl that I lost my virginity to [and I hope she did with me]. She was in my eyes a very sexy girl who wore all the clothes that I liked to see my females wearing. Stockings, high heels, tight tops, short skirts, etc along with long flowing blonde hair, we certainly experimented with our sexual awareness with all methods in all places at any time. Eventually later in that same year my brothers affair was brought to light resulting in the pair of them running off together to a far away place. During the same time my mother was also having an affair with a married man resulting in them also running off, but not before she had sold our house. As all of this was blowing up, I had decided to move out of the house and get myself some digs in the local transport café, as the rows at home were getting too unbearable. What a culture shock that was, when I was shown my room at my new abode to my astonishment there were seven beds in one room. " Pick out which one you want" said the old man who owned the café " before all the drivers come in" and true to his words later that evening I was sharing my room with six lorry drivers, most of which snored like troupers no matter how drunk they were. Every evening thereafter 6 new drivers occupied those same beds. The only major problem that I could see was the fact that the cost of my new lodgings was four pounds four shillings per week and I was only bringing home about £3 per week [depending on weather conditions as we were not allowed to lay bricks in heavy rain]. As my brother had by now ran off with his new found lady friend the band had also stopped, so there was no extra cash from that source. I didn't dare tell the owner of the café about my predicament, instead I thought I would wait until Friday when I get my pay packet, and upon my return home that evening just give him my unopened wages and wait to see what his reaction will be, and take it from there. At least I will get 5 nights sleep and food in the meantime so this I did. When I arrived back to the café that Friday evening, Pop the name every one called the owner said to me whilst looking over the top of his glasses, "before you sit down for your meal in my office now". I had already told him that I would be paying my tab on Friday evenings and he was used to being paid by every one first thing after breakfast was a bit anxious to get my cash. Oh well I thought I will soon find out now what's going to happen to me. He sat behind his desk still wearing his dirty white apron, got down this big black cash book, opened the page to that date and said " right four pounds four shillings please and that takes you up to next Monday." I reached into my back pocket took out my unopened pay pack and tossed it on the desk in front of him, he picked it up looked at it, then opened it counted the money within, just in case there was more inside than what was printed on the front. After realising that's all that was there was looked at me over his glasses again with a scouring stare and said. "You little bastard you knew that you wasn't

going to be able to pay all your keep, didn't you?
" " Yes pop I did " I replied " what else can I
do? I can only give you every thing I have got I
have no more. If you say that the four pounds
four shillings takes me up to Monday, then kick
me out now and we should be about quits." He
looked back at his book, put his hand to his
mouth whilst making a humming sound, reached
across the desk and picked up a fresh apron,
threw it at me and said right you little fu~~
ker from now on you can work in the kitchen
after work and week ends to make the rest of
your keep up, now go and eat your fu~~ing tea.
He was on old man, slightly crippled from the
second world war, ex Londoner, with language
befitting to any building site, but most of all he
had a heart of gold, and I was now in permanent
residence for some time to come.

In the event of my girlfriends mother being
absent along with my brother, I was not greeted
with great enthusiasm by her father at his
house, when calling for her, coupled with the
fact that I was working in the evenings thus
giving us less time together, put a strain on the
relationship. As expected she calmly announced
one evening that she was seeing someone else,

and that she wanted to finish our relationship forthwith. I suppose I could see her point after all there is no future in a relationship when you could be married to your stepfather's brother, or me going out with my step niece come to that, so we parted on a reasonably friendly basis. With my new home being somewhat busy along with sharing my bedroom with 6 strangers, I had no privacy at all, and certainly could not get dressed no matter how much I wanted to. Even though I had managed to pinch a few pairs of my ex girlfriend's stockings, the only time I was alone was on week ends when most of the lorry drivers were home, but Pop used to open the café at midnight on a Friday and Saturday to catch all the dance crowds on their way home. As you well know it is very difficult to get staff to work those hours, so that's where I came to the fore. By the time we closed at about 2-30 am then washed up, cleaned the floors and toilets ready for the next morning, I was pretty tired, especially after a days work on the building site. Getting dressed was the last thing on my mind before falling in a deep sleep, so again I had to keep those feelings suppressed. One day I would tell myself I will have a place of my own then I can do what I want, and the words my father used to drum into us rang in my ear work for what you want; and so I did.

As time went by my enthusiasm at work as a bricklayer was beginning to pay off, and my speed had definitely increased. As a result I felt quite confident to go out and look for work as a sub contractor, and to be paid on a pre arranged price for your work and not by the hour, that way the more you do the more you get paid. I was certainly no stranger to hard work, so off I went, and found advertised in the local weekly paper an advert for small gang of bricklayers wanted to build a bungalow. I phoned in response, was told the price was £280 to build from damp course to top out including the chimneystack. This included the provision of a cement mixer and the erection of supplied scaffold. I accepted and arranged to start on the coming Monday. There was only one problem this bungalow was 30 miles away, how on earth am I going to get there, easy I thought I have to employ a labourer/hod carrier so employ one with a car. I was still only 16 and not yet old enough to drive, so I knew such a chap with whom I had previously worked and was told that he was looking for work, so I called to see him as I knew where he lived, he accepted, so problem solved.

When we arrived on site on the Monday morning and met the site agent face to face for the first time his first words to me were " how old are you?" "Twenty one", I said in the deepest voice I could make. He just looked and said nothing, showed us the foundations where the bungalow was to be built, where all the necessary materials were, and left us to it. Now I know that any foreman worth his salt will be able to tell within a couple of hours whether I was any good or not, so I had something to prove and got stuck in. Sure enough after about 2 hours he came back to look over my work, he scrutinised it from all angles, then winked at me saying, "you will do."

We stayed there and built the bungalow and another one as well, having my 17th birthday half way through the contract, but I never told him that. When we finished building the first bungalow, by placing the chimney pot on top of the recently built stack, I climbed down the scaffolding, walked across to the other side of the unfinished road, and just stared with pride at my latest achievement. After a few minutes of silence, I burst into floods of tears, as my thoughts had turned to my father, and wishing with all my heart that he could be stood along side me this very second, and to put his strong arm around me and say" well done son". For all I ever wanted was to make my father proud of me. Even to this very day, whenever I finish my latest building project, I still have the same ritual, with those same thoughts, resulting in the same outcome with a tearful eye, but always in private. With the good money I was now earning, I was in a position to pay for my digs in full, great I thought time to myself. How wrong I was poor old Pop had come to depend on me working those awkward shifts, so I couldn't let him down, after all he had looked after me when I needed help, and in more ways than one. He always made sure I went to work with 10 cigarettes, and a few shillings in my pocket for emergencies so it was now my turn to pay back his kind actions, But I did get my own single bedded room, privacy at last.

It was time to get a car with my hard earned wages, and on the way to work in the early mornings had past a small country garage with an old Rover 12 on the forecourt with a sign saying 'For Sale £50' stuck to the windscreen. That was a lot of money in those days, the weekly national average wage being approximately £18. I remembered my dad having one of those in the earlier struggling years when he was working his way back to the top, and being car mad, begging him to let me have a go at driving it on the old airfield where we often went. As dad let my older brother have a drive, he succumbed to my pleas and sat me behind the wheel whilst he worked the foot pedals. Easy I thought after all I have been driving dumpers on the building site since I was 10 years old. On the following Friday evening when returning from work with my recent weeks pay packet, we stopped at the garage to look at this black monster [they were all black in those days]. I said to my hod carrier, who I am sure by now was fed up with all the driving to and from work in his car "when the bloke who owns the garage comes over to give us his sales pitch, pick as much fault with the car as you can" [remembering my dad doing the same]."That wont be very hard to do its falling to fu***ng bits any way", was his immediate reply. " Oh and kick the tyres as well, that always seems to do the trick!" So as he approached we sprung into action, I picked so many faults with the car that I nearly put myself off buying it! I think he got so fed up with all our criticism, and by now in need of his evening meal, just said "alright how much will you give me for it then". "40 quid and that's my last offer" I said. With that said he shook my hand and I was the proud owner of a Rover 12.

We managed to get it back to the café where after seeing it Pop said "what the f##k have you bought that for, bloody old thing." "Wheels Pop" I said " I am going to pass my test in this, then I wont need to depend on any one taking me to work, I will have my own transport." Seeing the sense in what I had just said he looked at me with a smile and said "park it round the back in the garage before any one sees it." That smile was Pop's sign of approval

Pop allowed me some time off in the evenings to have some driving lessons with any body I could find who had a full license, and told me to put in for my test as soon as possible as there is a long waiting list. This I did, and lo and behold within the week had a letter offering me a date in 2 weeks time through a cancellation. "I have only had 3 lessons Pop" I said " well get as many as you can between now and the test, and don't worry if you don't pass use it as a lesson and gain experience from it". This I did, and passed my test on the first attempt.

Well there is no stopping me now I thought, and as an added bonus I now have a back seat, somewhere that I can have complete privacy, providing I park up well out of the way. The only problem that I could see was the car itself, although it was a good car for me to learn in, and get to work with, it wasn't much of a bird puller. So with the good money I was able to earn by working longer hours and the odd week end, I bought myself a mark 7 Jaguar silver grey. My dad used to have a mark 9 the same shape and style but with a slightly larger engine, but hey this was near enough for me. Can you imagine the situation I was in, a young lad only 17 years old, not bad looking, with a Jag, living in a small town, where every one knows each other, a few bob in his pocket, and most importantly lots of single females, most of which were readily available. What a reputation I soon acquired, most of it true. I wont tell you what Pop said when I first arrived home to the café, and proudly parked my Jag outside the front of the building for all to see. When he had calmed down a little, and the air wasn't so blue, in my reply to being asked, " why did you buy that?" "Well wasn't it you Pop that said the last one was a load of rubbish". Pop for once was silent, but the scouring look he gave me as he hobbled away on his walking stick, spoke volumes.

By now my work was going really well, after finishing the two bungalows, I had managed to get some work closer to home, where I built four houses on an estate which was nearing completion. The large gang of bricklayers, who had done the majority of the site, left these last 4 houses to secure a large contract for themselves with another contractor. So being a small fry as it where, I was the perfect candidate to step in and finish off the site, especially as I had told the site agent that there were three of us; two bricklayers and one hod carrier. When he asks where the other man is on our first day I will tell him he's on holiday or something like that. By the time he realises that there is only one bricklayer and the hod carrier, it will be too late I will have one of the pairs half way up and he will be committed to keep me. Especially as in those days we were having a boom in the construction industry and tradesmen where strong demand, and true to my plans that's exactly what happened. Not only did I build the two pairs of houses, but also built several blocks of garages, various retaining and boundary walls, along with most of all the internal partition walls throughout the whole site, all in all making it a very lucrative steady contract, my speed as a bricklayer, was matching my quality, and I was therefore gaining a good reputation in my local area.

Pop's health was deteriorating and so decided to sell the café and go to live with his son many miles away. On his last day as owner, a few of the locals and I put on a farewell party for him. Later that day when the festivities had died down, and just before the arrival of the new owners, Pop took me in his office for the last time. He hung up his apron, sat behind that rickety old desk, and offered me a seat alongside him. We started to reminisce over my last 2 -3 years living in the café, and how I had progressed from a snotty nosed school boy, [his very words] to a man who has got a nice little business going. He appreciated the times when I had seeked his advice, and mostly took it, then told me. "You are not a bad lad at all, you are not afraid of hard work, you have got a good pair of hands on you, matched with an old head on young shoulders, keep at it, and you will make it one day". He then shook my hands, and for the first time since I had known him Pop put his arm around my shoulder and cried like a baby. " I am going to miss you Pop," I said whilst trying to hold back my own tears. "Not half as much as I am going to miss you, you little fu##er" were his parting words.

With the new owners now in place there was no need for my services in the running of the café, as there was a family now doing Pops old job and each one of them had been delegated their duties. Great news for me I now could go it with my mates to dances, get drunk, and do all those things that young men do. We certainly had our fair share of all the fore mentioned, and I in particular, along with the huge back seat of my Jag, went into overtime with all the available females within a 15 mile radius. Single, divorced, young, old, or married, it made no difference; I was making up for lost time. Its funny but even though I was enjoying the manly experiences, I still had the urge to get dressed into those feminine silky clothes, and the more conquests I achieved, the more those urges would increase. This really started to worry me now, as after all here I am a man in every sense, not a bad looking one, can get more or less any women I want, I have a healthy sexual appetite, I certainly don't have any inclination towards men whatsoever, so why on earth do I feel the need to get dressed into women's clothes. I really could not come to terms with it, so to compensate would find more willing females to fulfil my desires, so a catch 22 situation was developing.

Time to get my own place, I thought, after all I can afford to rent somewhere, and the café is just not the same without Pop, and the back seat of the Jag was showing great signs of wear. I found a nice 2-bedroom cottage, and the rent was well within my means. My reputation with the females was soon the topic of conversation on my new street. With all the comings and goings of women of certain [shall we say] less than reputable variety, along with some very irate fathers and the occasional husband knocking my door in the middle of the night, I soon woke that sleepy little street up in that small town, but I always seemed to be able to avoid confrontation and talk my way out of trouble. Although once or twice I had to resort the boxing skills my dear old dad had taught me as a youngster, along with another one of his sayings" never look for trouble son, let trouble find you, but make sure you can handle it when it does". I suppose I was no different than any other healthy, normal, young lad, who was a little bit wild, in those mid sixties.

Never the less I thought it best if I slow things down a bit, and with the opportunity of having my own place, and with mail order shopping becoming more popular, decided to pursue my feminine urges, which were by now at boiling point. So I scoured the daily newspapers for a wig, and found what I thought looked ok, signed up to a catalogue store, and sent off for some of the latest fashions, which caught my eye. Shoes were a bit of a disaster as I took a size 9; the largest size available in the book was 8, so it was cramped feet or nothing, hoping they would stretch in time. Make up was also a bit of a problem, so I had to buy those sets for beginners, usually for little girls, but that's ok I thought as I have no intentions of going out it will be good enough for me. Looking back I can only imagine what a sight I must have looked, still when looking in the mirror at the time I thought I looked good, and that's all that mattered. One great advantage to my dressing escapades was the fact that when dressed, I really enjoyed doing feminine things, such as cooking, washing and ironing clothes, and generally cleaning the house up, and at times it really needed it. As you can imagine a young lad living on his own was not always house proud, these dressing events usually took place at week ends and upon my return to work on the Monday mornings, I would feel guilty and disgusted with myself. Yet when I was dressed as Susie, feeling proud of Peter, for he was the breadwinner in her eyes, providing her clothes, and the roof over her head. Even so the whole affair would give me great cause for concern, I was definitely becoming two separate people, with each side being completely opposite to the other, a pattern which was to emerge more clearly in the future. During this period I never told any one of my shameful secret, for fear of ridicule, especially as by now, I had achieved great success with my contracting works, and was employing half a dozen men, all of whom relied on me as their boss to keep the work coming in, and successfully negotiate with the main contractor for the weekly wages.

Chapter 6
BOY TO MAN?

By the time I reached 20 years old, I was employing approximately 30 men, and had just successfully completed a large hotel for John Laing, I was on my sixth Jag a mark 2 3.8 saloon in pure white, a proper bird puller. How I never killed myself in that car I will never know, there was only one speed [flat out] having crashed most of the Jags previously through my one and only speed, I really was lucky to be alive, but still a Jag fanatic. In those days there were no speed restrictions, so once outside the 30-mile limit it was foot down. I can vividly remember one Saturday afternoon driving to Bournemouth for a week end in the bright lights, coming up behind a police car [a Wolsey 6 80] with his bells ringing obviously answering an emergency call, and thinking to myself he isn't going very fast [about 90] so I passed him. You should have seen the black look they gave me as I sped past doing about 110 mph, they didn't stop me [well they couldn't catch me] I suppose, but never received anything in the post neither, needless to say though I didn't do that again, just in case.

But things were definitely on the up; I had built up a really good wardrobe in my second bedroom [out of the way from prying females' eyes]. I had bought some better make up, some shoes that fitted, even a pair of leather boots with a heel, and I was getting brave enough to buy my own stockings and tights which were taking over from stockings, as the mini skirt was now well in fashion. Oh how I loved that mini skirt, all that gorgeous leg on display, its funny but most men who were around at that time will tell you that even bad legs looked good in a mini skirt. So all in all every thing was going on quite nicely, this is too good to be true. And it was, just after my 21st birthday I had taken a contract to build 8 multi- storey blocks of flats, employing about 40 men to assist in the construction. It was at that time when the trade unions were trying to stop all of the self employed workers linked to the construction trade by encouraging them to join the union. My men were split into 2 separate gangs and I had entrusted a long-term employee of mine with one of the gangs as a foreman, whilst I looked after the other. All was well until one day when we were approached by two officials of the unions who were talking to my men whilst working, and going from man to man, until eventually they had stopped most of them from laying bricks. Well I was not going to stand for that, so I approached them and said. "I pay them their wages and whilst I do so they will earn them, so if you wish to talk to them do so in your time not mine". The two of them walked over to the side and chatted amongst themselves, I then asked my men in turn what their views were, and the reply was unanimous in the fact that they wished to remain self-employed. They did not want to join the unions and wanted to be left alone, good enough for me as I thought. The 2 officials then approached me and started to preach their gospel to me on how to run my business according to their rules. I took this for so long and warned them on several occasions to leave me and my workforce alone, but to no avail the more I asked them to leave the more persistent they became, until in the end I decked the pair of them. This was the biggest mistake I have ever made. I remember well as they laid on the ground and them looking back at me saying "that's going to cost you your job". So it did, six weeks after that event I was declared bankrupt, through being black listed with all of the suppliers of materials who were supplying me, who were already under the control of the unions. The main contractor who had already made me sign a contract with them to keep at least 35 men on site at all times to keep the controlling majority would not release me from my contract, so the only way out for me was to prove insolvency. I had to watch all my savings go until I had nothing then make myself bankrupt. Looking back I can't help thinking that the main contractor and the trade unions were using me like a pawn in some large business game of chess.

I lost everything I had worked so hard for, the only thing that I was left with was my tools and my clothes, gone was my car, and the van, all my furniture [as the cottage was unfurnished], television, and any personal effects that was worth anything. All of this knocked me for six at the time. I had to give up my cottage, and find some more digs to live in and get a job working for someone else. I was not allowed a bank account, so I had to be paid in cash, no more cheques, and of course with no transport the new job had to be local. Another lesson in life that I learnt at that time, was that living in a small town where every one knows you, whilst they so called like to see someone get on in this world, they like it better when you crash down.

I don't know why it was, but I seemed to blame my feminine side for the downfall and Susie in particular. Strange that, as in reality she had done nothing at all, how could it be her fault. Never the less I took all of Susie's clothes out in the garden one dark evening, and burnt the lot. I couldn't take them with me to my new digs [a public house] as there was no where to hide them, I told myself, but deep down it was my revenge to Susie for the situation that I now found myself in. Looking back I suppose I wanted to blame any body but myself, and as she was the nearest person to me she got it. Well I got a job with a local builder at £18 per week a big come down, but I said to myself; I have done it once I will do it again. Though next time I will do things differently, and my old dad's words rang in my ear' work for what you want' .So it was head down and arse up as we say in the bricklaying world and so I did. Word soon spread around the local builders about my downfall, and one-day I was approached by a relatively new builder to go and work for him on piecework. He was willing to pay me cash to overcome my banking problems, this I did and soon found the old Peter again I needed a confidence boost and this was it. Before long I was in a position to buy a car, not much an old Ford Consul but it was transport, and as my new work was all over the place it was much needed. Now whether it was because I was at low ebb in my life or not I don't know but it was at this time that I met my wife to be. I do know that I was very lonely after being on my own since the age of 16, and I definitely wanted to have a family life again. After all I was approaching 22 years old but after the last 6 years I felt 32 and I did not want to be left on the shelf, especially as most of the people at my age in that area where already married. And one night when I was out to a local dance with an ex workmate of mine, I met this gorgeous girl and once again fell madly in love and lust. She was nearly 18 and I was nearly 22, we were married in 3 weeks exactly to the day we first met, by special license on a Saturday. I remember on my wedding night lying in bed [after performing my honeymoon ritual] thinking what the hell have I done. Too late now I have got to stand by my sentiments, and the very next day went to work on the Sunday with my new wife to lay some drain pipes, and god bless her she helped as best she could.

Nine months after more or less to the day she gave birth to my one and only child a son, so I must have done something right on that honeymoon night.

When we first got married we lived with her mother, [well I couldn't smuggle her in my digs] my mother in law and I got on famously, and although she had brought up 7 kids on her own she always spoilt me. I very often played on that, by telling her what my favourite meal was knowing she would cook that for my evening meal after a days work, she really did have a heart of gold, god bless her.

During that first 9 months of married life, up to the birth of my son, life really was a struggle. We needed to get a place of our own, and as my wages were not as good as they had been, due to the winter months which meant shorter hours and lots of wet time. Plus I was still picking myself up from my collapsed business, but we finally did get a 2 bed second storey flat, in a town about 7 miles from my mother in laws home. Not too far to get those special meals, however it was unfurnished and we had nothing, but with help from good old mother in law, a few other friends and the rest of the wife's family, we moved into a very sparse cold flat. But at least it was a place of our own, and it gave me more incentive to get back on top again if only to get a comfortable armchair, as between my wife and I we only had one hard wood rocking chair, and one deck chair, on bare wooden floor boards. As the weeks went by we would buy something from the second hand shop near by every week from whatever spare cash was left from that week's wages, and eventually we got there just in time for the birth of our son. Shortly after the birth we had the chance to rent a nice bungalow with lovely gardens and a private drive, which we thought would be a good place for our son to grow up in, as the flat had no garden, being right on the main trunk road, and a very steep set of stairs to negotiate. Being in the same town we could still be only 7 miles from mother in law [the baby sitter]. We both really enjoyed living in that bungalow as it was semi rural, nice and private and very quiet, work was picking up and we were definitely improving our with our finances, I had even bought a mark 9 Jag in really good condition for peanuts. The garage who were selling it declared the fact that there was a serious fault with the automatic gear-box, saying that it was going to be very costly to repair, resulting in them slashing the price of the car to compensate. Having had so many Jags, and not always being able to afford garage repair prices, being mechanically minded and inquisitive to the workings of most machinery bought it and took a chance. To my delight when underneath this car and covered in oil I found the problem in a flash, just a wire had come off a solenoid, what a bargain that was.

It was also at this time that the gorgeous hot pant fashion came to light. As if mini skirts weren't enough the male population now had two lots of distraction to contend with. I for one nearly crashed my car on several occasions, suffering from the inability to return my head to a forward position when driving past some gorgeous female wearing the said item. Fortunately for me, my wife who incidentally retained her young perfectly shaped figure and slender legs, after the birth of our son, as a result bought several pairs of hot pants. One pair in particular was of the stretch type [very handy for me] and I have a fond memory of on one occasion after taking my wife and son to her mothers one Saturday, for a weekend of mother and nanny bonding. Left alone in the bungalow until the Sunday lunchtime, I slipped on these hot pants. Which then led in turn, to trying on some of her tights, then a top, and finally every thing I could get my hands on that would fit, including make up and perfume stayed all evening dressed, even sleeping with it all on. The minute I started to first touch those items on that Saturday, all my female and cross dressing tendencies came flooding back in droves, and there was no way I could have stopped them, they just had to be fulfilled.

This first little escapade led to many other convenient weekends of family bonding for me to satisfy my feminine side, and my wife was always pleased to see a well-vacuumed and polished bungalow on her return. Unfortunately for me she started to suspect me of having an affair, and accusing me of cleaning the home to impress some other woman, how wrong she was. Eventually I had to confess my desire to get dressed into women's clothes. And after a night of convincing talk to her she finally believed me saying" well in future don't use my clothes, as you will stretch them out of shape tell me what sort of thing you like and I will get some just for you". Although she accepted my cross dressing she never really understood, I suppose come to that neither did I, but because of her lack of understanding, it also failed to gain her approval I didn't, and never have held that against her. Even I still to this very day don't fully understand the reasons for my crossdressing and probably never will, I suppose some shrink somewhere will have an answer but that will only be an assumption.

With my new found shopping partner my own wardrobe started to grow again, and as fashions had moved on somewhat since my last collection it was certainly nice for me to keep abreast with the latest. My wife allowed me the privacy at weekends to fulfil my needs, but she never really liked to see me dressed, so all of my experiences were done in solitude. But with my thoughts always wandering into realms of fantasy of wondering what it would be like to be a woman in various situation, How you would feel whilst being admired by a man, and how indeed you would act to attract a man. After all I had been on the other side of the coin on many occasions, and as a man I knew what I liked to have in response to my needs, but what was it like for them. During these moments of fantasy would try to imagine my feelings as a woman under the same circumstances. I would even in the evenings when darkness fell, walk out side our bungalow around the garden paths, just to listen to the sound of my high heels clinking on the concrete path, and the feel of that evening chilled air on my nylon clad legs was fabulous and still is to this day. Its funny but it seems to be silly little things like that what really stick in my mind, and since my early days of dressing to now, I have talked to many other transvestites, and they all have said that they too shared very many similar experiences.

Chapter 7
IN BUSINESS

Another advantage to being married, was the fact that my wife, who played an active part in my business as bookkeeper, was able to have a bank account, thus enabling me to engage in lucrative contracts on a more professional basis. This resulted in a steady growth of generated income, which in turn assisted me in paying off my previous bankruptcy and obtaining a complete discharge. Freedom at last, I could now operate without one hand tied behind my back, although I had learnt my trade as a bricklayer, I had also in my earlier days worked with a lot of stone, both natural and reconstructed, and found these materials far more interesting and financially rewarding. I decided that this was the way forward, as the more expensive type of properties were built of these materials, it seemed obvious to me that the price to build them would be greater than that of bricks, and so it was, not only more lucrative but also more specialised. I stuck to my guns and decided that this had to be the way forward, especially as there was no one else in our area offering these services on a large scale. After a couple of years and a few ups and downs I managed to secure a large contract in an up and coming town on the south coast about 15 miles away from our bungalow. Time for another move, get nearer the action, to keep my finger well and truly on the pulse, I advertised for specialist stone layers, offering good rates of pay and slowly but surely increased my workforce, working alongside of them leading from the front. We successfully completed the large contract and gained a good reputation for quality workmanship. Word soon spread throughout the construction industry in that part of the country, and we eventually became sought after by some of the larger contractors in the U K. As a result of our ability to produce quality crafted workmanship on schedule, we were nominated by 3 county councils for any large public contracts in those counties. Now the big boys in our industry were coming to me, more so on the civil engineering side, and our portfolio soon boasted large stone built bridges over rivers for new trunk roads, along with all the stone fly overs, new supermarkets, sea defence granite walling, river diversion and flood elevation works all in natural stone. My work force increased to over 100 strong, and soon found myself working full time in the companies office just to keep up with all the tendering for the incoming work, as well as chasing all the existing contractors for their payments due. With all the pressure of running this large business [which was by now a limited company] and employing 110 men, my marriage was under immense strain and was showing signs of cracking. We as a family did not have the time to take proper holidays, as I was working 7 days per week from dawn to dusk, and was only seeing my wife under office circumstances, and even then we would be at loggerheads over some crisis or another. I was approaching 30 years old and my company was turning over nearly one million pounds pr year. I was responsible for putting the food on the table to the families of my entire 110 workforce, and the pressure was immense. My only source of release came through my dressing experiences, which in turn were being extremely limited, not only through lack of time available, but also with a growing inquisitive son.

My wife and I decided to separate with me moving out leaving the house and all its contents to her. As her main role in life was to bring up our son, we decided would take on a new full time secretary in the office, enabling my wife to work only 3 days per week. This took some of the strain out of our relationship, after all we still had the business together, and more importantly we were the best of friends, and wanted to stay that way. I rented a large house within walking distance from my wife's home, and only a stones throw away from the office. From that day onwards we never argued again, and have remained the best of friends to this very day. We even started to take holidays together when time allowed, it seemed we couldn't live together and yet couldn't live apart. I found more time for my dressing, and she found more time for my shopping, she would even come over to my house on the odd occasion and let me cook us both a nice meal whilst I would be dressed usually like a tart. Whereupon we would both fall about in fits of laughter, but I did taking the mickey out of myself whilst dressed, and still do, it helped me to come to terms with my dressing needs, and to accept it on a lighter note, and it certainly helped her. Its funny but when I got myself all tarted up, the pressures that I was facing with my business as Peter would just vanish, it really was a tremendous form of release, and my wife could see that for herself. She would say to me "some men like to play golf, some men like to the pub and get drunk, but you like to be a tart, so what, I would rather see you as a tart than a drunken golfer". All of which helped me to accept and come to terms with the fact that I am a transvestite.

We still keep in contact with each other even after 40 years and very often meet up. Either as Peter or as Susie and we still end up in fits of laughter, usually over the length of my skirts, which seem to get shorter, as the years get longer but as I tell her "if you've got it flaunt it".

ALL went well for a good 6 years, the business grew, and so did Susie's wardrobe. She even dared to go out one evening dressed to the hilt for just a little drive in the car. Only venturing to go out when dark, and only then for about a 5-mile round trip, but what a thrill that was. The excitement that I experienced for those few minutes was both electrifying and terrifying especially when pulling up at a set of traffic lights in the centre of town. Whilst waiting for the lights to change colour, a car pulled up on my near side filled with young bullish males, all shouting lewd remarks to what they thought was a single girl travelling alone. Those lights seemed to take forever to change, and for the first time in my life I experienced just how intimidating life can be for single females in a so called mans world whilst travelling alone in the dark evenings. Since that evening I have never copied the actions of those young men. Even so the memories of that evening have stayed with me to this very day.

As a businessman I had become shrewd and careful or so I thought, making sure not to put all my eggs in one basket. I had split my firm into three separate gangs with each gang working on a different contract for a different main contractor, that way no one firm could bring me down, they could make life difficult for a while but not destroy me. Then early one Monday morning I received a phone call from one of my foreman to say that they couldn't get into the site with it being all locked up. There were signs on the gates saying' all who are connected with [then the name of the main contractor] please contact the official receiver'. I then knew straight away that they had gone under. I told the foreman to take all of the men to the two other remaining sites and share the workforce evenly, until I could make further arrangements. I rushed straight to the office to find out how much we were owed. In those days it was common practise to work on site for four weeks, then a quantity surveyor would measure your work to value, and then a cheque would be issued taking another four weeks to arrive. So if you have got say 35 men working for 8 weeks times 3 that's a lot of money you have to carry at any one time, and as sub-contractors we are not classed as preferential creditors, in other words you have no chance of getting your money. When I reached the office I discovered that their last cheque was late in coming so it was more like 9 weeks money due. I had to call in my company's accountant in for a crisis meeting, where he informed me that we as a company had no option but to follow suit and call in a liquidator on behalf of our company. I argued the point and said that if I as managing director was to sell all my personal assets to raise cash for the company we could survive and pull through. It would mean perhaps having to stand off several of our workforce until a replacement contract could be won, but never the less we could survive. The accountant advised against this action, but I was not prepared to go down without a fight. So I sold every asset I had and we just about covered the loss, but my e type jag was gone, and so was my new cabin cruiser boat, along with all my personal savings. Phew that was a close one I thought just about pulled out of that one. Then out of the blue within 6 weeks of the first contractors closure the remaining two went bust within 3 weeks of each other, and between the three of them they took my firm for thousands of pounds. We then had no option but to follow suit, and so I called in a liquidator and closed down my company. With the event of previously selling all my own personal assets I was left with absolutely nothing, just my old hand tools which for the last 6 years or so were left in my garden shed gathering rust.

Back to square one here I was at 36 years old with nothing but a bag full of rusty old tools, so I went back to piece work bricklaying. Done it before do it again was my attitude. I soon found work as I still had a good reputation for my skills, and with an ex employee from my old firm we built a large private house in the country for a professional gentleman who worked in the oil industry. It was good for me to get back to my skills, it gave me time to think and readjust to my new surroundings, and to my future direction. I decided that small was indeed beautiful and I was not going to get such a large workforce again.too many headaches keep my destiny in my own two hands and not to let any one else in the future control my destiny.

Things went quite well and my work partner and I secured a good few lucrative private contracts and made a very good living for ourselves. I slowly replaced my assets with a really nice car, a Jenson interceptor series 3, and bought a new speedboat. As for Susie, well her wardrobe grew especially with having more spare time only working 5 days per week and being home for evening meals every night. I still kept my rented Victorian house, and even sub let out a couple of rooms on the third floor for extra income. At the same time I was approached by an old friend who was working part time on the doors of a new night-club in our region, who asked me to join him on the doors as a bouncer. There had been a lot of trouble in this club, and no body wanted to take the job as second bouncer. As my friend put it unless I took the job he himself was going to pack it in. "I am brave" he said but not that bloody brave to stand there on my own with 600 drunken revellers to control, so me being me I took the job. The extra money came in very handy working 4 nights a week at £40 per night, and the added bonus was all those gorgeous girls with those skimpy clothes [oh god]. The funny thing with it all was that I would go to work in the evening with my penguin suite on but under that would be my stockings, suspender, and frilly knickers. I often wondered when throwing out some local so called hard nut, who when outside would give me abuse for the way in which I had thrown him out, if only you knew the truth that you have just been taken down by someone wearing women's clothes. Still in the two years I worked there nobody ever got the better of me to find out [thank god]

It was whilst working in the nightclub that I met my second wife, a very attractive girl 19 years my junior. Although I thought at the time it was love at first sight, I now see that it was more of an ego boost trip, when you are 37 and have an 18-year-old girlfriend it does make you feel special at the time. We soon lived together after a short courtship, and as quick as we lived together I also told her about my dressing habits, she was most intrigued about the whole thing, and so one Sunday evening

I suggested that I should cook us both a nice meal whilst being dressed, and to keep the atmosphere level it would be nice for her to get dressed into something smart but sexy as well. This we did and that was the first time I ever made love to a woman whilst dressed, it was fantastic, not only for me but also for her, it was a new experience for both of us. One that was going to be repeated on many occasions. When we first moved in together I always told her that I had no intentions of ever getting married again, but she had other ideas, and by the time she was 21 I gave in to her wants and we were married. Its funny but on my wedding day I told my friend who was my best man, that the marriage wouldn't last.

Although we had another 6 years together by the time the end came it was due, the last 2-3 years we were definitely growing apart. With me approaching 47 and her still only 27 with all her life ahead of her the writing was on the wall. Even so I still took the split up very much to heart, as I loved her so dearly, but I promised her that I would let go and not bother her. That's exactly what I did, and to this day I have had no further contact with her and never likely to, and where ever she may be I still wish her the very best of luck and health. There are no hard feelings at all, and I hope she can say the same. Even so it took me a good 2 years to come to terms with my loss, for she had showed not only me but Susie also a lot of love and affection.

Eventually after moving about all over the place with work and itchy feet I finished up back in Bournemouth, where I got myself a nice little bachelor pad right in the middle of the red light area, what a coincidence. After a while I began to settle again and got myself a good job doing small private contracts, extensions, repairs, alterations etc.

I was starting to get established again, I employed 1 full time staff and several self employed occasional workers. I also made a couple of good friends and we would go out and do the town whenever we could.

We even joined some modern jive dance clubs, what a time we had there with all those lonely separated females. I think the ratio was about 3 females to every 1 male, [good odds in my book] but more importantly a good insight into all those fashions again. When the girls did that fast spin and their dresses would fly out straight, you could see just who was wearing the stockings and who wasn't. Very often if either of us took a fancy to one particular female, the other one would ask her for a dance, make sure that you give her a good spin, whilst the other one looks to see what she is wearing, simple but it worked.

All of this new and exciting activity seemed to encourage the femme side of me, and I found myself getting more and more comfort from my private dressing moments, along with refreshing my wardrobe. Although most of my clothes were kept in carrier bags well hidden in the back of a cupboard just in case I ever brought back to the flat any of those dancing girls, especially with having an insight to how a woman thinks. Naturally having an inquisitive mind like I know you women have, I thought it best to hide them. As for living in the red light district, this would fascinate me, as I had a large bay window to my flat, with frontal views and net curtains. This enabled me to study the ladies of the night plying their trade unnoticed. I was really amazed how unattractive, overweight, and untidy most of the ladies were; I just could not see how a man could actually go with one of these girls, no matter how desperate he may be. I know I certainly couldn't, never the less it still fascinated me watching through the net curtains just how it all went on. No sooner had they been picked up in a passing car, they were back again within 20 minutes, all over and done with and richer in the bag by whatever they had charged. I talked to several neighbours about what I was witnessing and explained my observations about their appearances. I was told that these were the girls that do this for drug money and they don't really care what they look like just as long as they get their £60 for the next fix. Good god I said £60 for 20 minutes for them ugly cows, I wouldn't do it even if they paid me £60. Well any one who is any good doesn't walk the streets. They advertise in the local papers as escorts and meet the clients at their own home or flat, and they get much more money, more like £150 for 1 hour, and its all done out of sight in a much more civilised way. That seemed a much better way to me plus it keeps the streets clear, and I was told its not illegal, especially if they declare their work to the inland revenue and pay taxes accordingly. This seemed to make much more sense to me, and when dressed I would imagine myself being in that position as a woman. What fun I could have and even make a living out of it, little did I know then that one day that's exactly what I would be doing.

Even though I was taking close order of what was happening on my own doorstep, I couldn't help but think that if I were a woman I would certainly do things different to them. I suppose I do have an advantage over the females, for being a man I know what another man is looking for and how to present myself for his needs. After all most men pretty much all like the same type of things, and I above all know that men only think with what they have in their trousers where women are concerned. Believe me that really is true. That is the time to catch them, it is then when you can control them to do almost anything you want, have them wrapped around your little finger so to speak. All of this nosy looking out of my window was a good learning curve for me to be put to practise in the near future.

Around this same time I even took up my old pastime of playing the drums again. After making contact with my old group members, we all agreed to meet up at a given rendezvous and spend a week together to practise our old skills, then book a studio and record our favourite 12 old 60s tracks onto a compact disk just for ourselves to keep for old time sake. What great fun we all had talking over all the good old times, I even got some session work from all of this recording on different cds for a singer songwriter, and to promote his new recording, played a few gigs. The first one being at an evening horse race meeting on the south coast, although I was very nervous to play in front of all those people again after 45 years, it was, after the first number, enormously exciting and all those old memories just came flooding back. We even had a couple of models who had been promoting some product at the races, jump up on the stage and dance to some of the old rock numbers we played. You can guess where my eyes were, I even had my faithful dog with me who incidentally would never leave my side, and would insist on lying right in front of my bass drum throughout the whole event, fast asleep. How he managed that I will never know. He even did this act throughout all of my recording sessions, much to the fear of the recording engineer who was afraid of him making a noise during a take, [he never did] but during our live gig at the races he drew the attention of the models. Take it from me a cute dog is definitely a good bird puller.

After that gig we went back to the Northeast to perform another outdoor venue. It was in the September on my birthday actually, and it was at this gig that I met my third wife. It was definitely love at first sight for both of us, I even sang lead, dedicating a number to her, in the second half of our performance, an old Eddie Cochran number Summertime Blues. Most unusual for me as I only ever sang on backing vocals, we men do the daftest of things where women are concerned, like I said men only think with one thing. When the evening was over, my new found love told me that she was just starting a weeks holiday, and I naturally asked her where she was going, nowhere was her reply," well how would you like to spend the week with me in Bournemouth?" I asked in a confident voice. "Oh yes", she said to my surprise. So early the next morning I picked her up at her house, and off we drove back to Bournemouth, in my old van with all my drum kit, a friend of mine who had come up from Bournemouth with me, and of course my old faithful dog.

It was whilst driving back that I suddenly remembered, that I had not hidden all my clothes some, mostly underwear and stockings had been left in my chest of drawers, and women being women this one in my van had brought enough clothes for a month not a week. Like all women she would be needing all of my wardrobe and drawer space to pack her mountain of clothes into, how was I going to get in first to on my own to clear my clothes out of sight? As luck would have it my friend lived next door to me so I suggested that we go into his place first for a cup of tea, whilst I go to mine and clear up the mess that I had left, as I had been in a hurry when going to perform the gig. She accepted this excuse saying, " I know what you men are like always untidy". I took all that on the chin just to get my few minuets of solitude to clear the way and it worked a treat. When I first suggested that she could spend the week with me I told her that I would be the proper gentleman and let her have the one and only bedroom to herself, and that I would sleep on the couch. True to my word that's exactly what I did. I think she was a little surprised that I kept my word, but I was careful not to push things too fast, as I really did think a lot of her. I think after 3 nights with her sleeping on her own she was beginning to worry that I didn't fancy her .So she, on the fourth night suggested that I share the bed with her, [I was beginning to think she would never ask]. BINGO I had cracked it; I had taken a few days off work myself, so that I could be with her for most of the week. I took her all around the local beauty spots, out for evening meals, and even took her to one of my dances, we really did fall in love with each other that week, which seemed to just fly by.

When I took her back to her hometown the following weekend, we agreed to meet in 2 weeks time, with me spending the weekend at her place. During the days leading up to that event I really had to think hard and long about my cross-dressing. I knew that I could not stop, yet I was in love with this woman, there was only one thing to do, and that was to tell her all about myself, and give her the opportunity to break away now before we get too involved and hurt even more. So on the weekend of our meet, I booked a table at a nice restaurant, and over a romantic meal told her every thing about my effeminate side right from the beginning. She seemed to take it all quite well considering and appreciated me being honest with her. I then suggested that when she next came to stay with me, in 2 weeks time, I will get myself dressed on the Saturday evening and cook us both a nice meal, then she can see Susie for herself. I told her we would both have a good laugh, I explained that I don't take it that seriously and very often laugh at myself and that I would make sure that she did see the funny side of it, as life is far too short to analyse this side of me to a point of misery. I am what I am so if you still love me after you have seen me, then lets use it to our advantage and have fun with it. This was met with an approving smile, and an anticipation of what was to come in a fortnight's time. "I cant wait to see what you look like" she said, and added that she always thought that something was different about me, as I seemed to understand women more than she had previously found with other men. This I took as a compliment, but I did point out that I did not have many clothes as I found it difficult to purchase my style and size with out embarrassment. She understood this, and said "don't worry shopping is my favourite pastime, I will soon get you sorted out". My heart was in my mouth, for this was far more than I could ever have hoped for. When the 2 weeks had finally arrived after what seemed like an eternity, I drove to her home on the Friday evening after work, arriving at approximately 10pm then after loading the car with all her weekend clothes, drove straight back to Bournemouth, getting back at about 2am. The next day my nerves were all on edge thinking of what was to come in the evening. We went shopping [for the evening food] and we talked all day of what was to come. All the time I was reassuring her that it would be a laugh and that she wasn't to be afraid to say whatever she wanted to and to laugh as much as she wished, because I certainly will laugh at myself, and I will make sure she does. As I was getting myself ready in the bathroom, and shaking like a leaf I was still not convinced that she would take it well. So I got out all of what I thought were my best clothes, put them on. Next I put on my make up to what I thought was looking good, placed my wig on, brushed it then took a last look at myself in the mirror. Looking back on reflection, I did not have a clue, I knew how a woman should look but to try and emulate that is another thing. I had on white shoes, with black tights, pink mini skirt, green top, make up that looked like a cross between a drunken women who had slept with it on all night then cried when seeing herself in the mirror, and Coco the clown. The wig on my head looked like a dead cat curled up. My wife to be was already dressed for the occasion and waiting for me in the living room for my grand appearance. There was no need for me to try and make her laugh, one look at me was enough, we both just simply fell to the floor in unstoppable fits of laughter, and although I cant speak for her, I literally wet my knickers and tights.

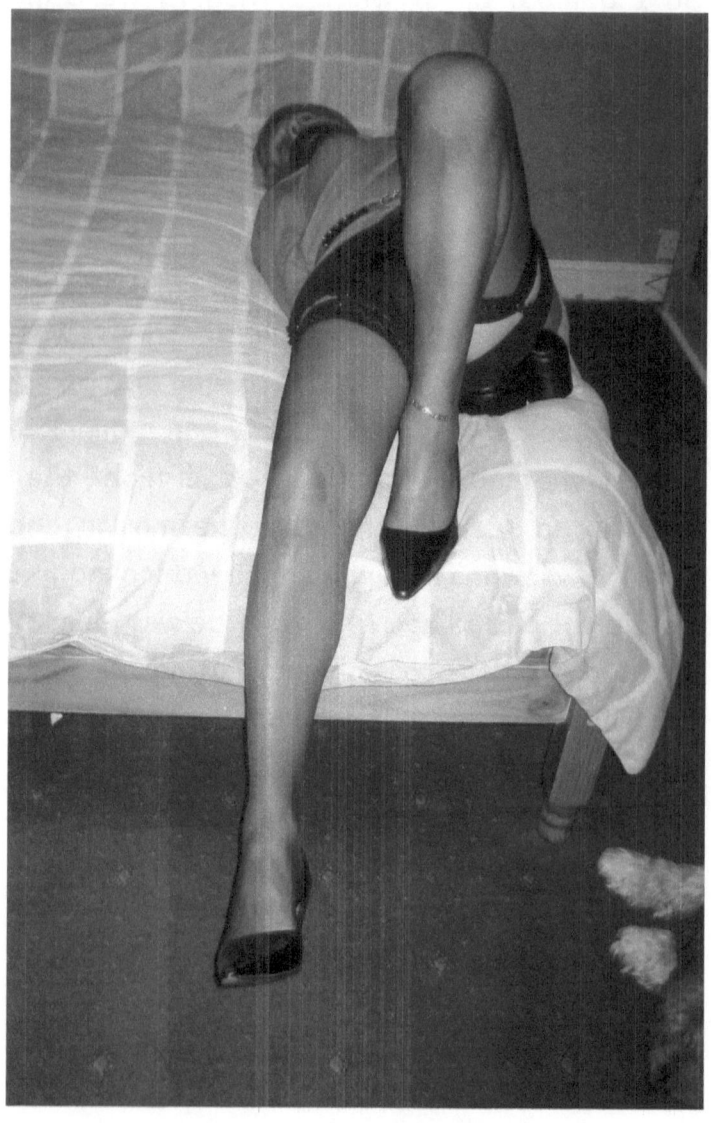

Chapter 8
TAKING OVER

After the laughter had finally stopped, we ate our by now cold meal and talked nearly all through the night. She said that if I were going to dress then she would take over with my style and buy what she thought was best for me, after all when it comes to shopping who better to have to spend your money on women's clothes than a woman. I was completely over the moon, and for the first time in my life did not feel ashamed with myself. That had been one of the most tormenting things with my cross dressing, not at the time of being dressed, but afterwards, usually the next day whilst at work I would reflect on my previous days actions and be thoroughly ashamed, believing that I was a freak. But now things were a lot different. I not only had a lover for Peter but a really good friend for Susie and lots of future shopping trips for new clothes, as my future wife had by now been all through my femme clothes discarding all that she thought was no good, which didn't leave a lot left. So every chance we got it was off to town and looking through all the charity shops we could find, and what some bargains there is to be had there, my wardrobe grew and grew.

By the time Christmas and the New Year [which was the millennium] had arrived, we were discussing moving in together, with her moving down to Bournemouth and in with me in my small flat. By this time I had taken on another small room to store not only my clothes but those of my future wife, and when she eventually moved in with me in early January it was a toss up on who had the most clothes. One of the first things she did when she moved in was to get rid of the dead cat wig and buy a new one from a ladies hairdresser, what a difference that made. Of course we still enjoyed our Saturday evenings in with Susie cooking a romantic meal for two with lots of wine, and even more laughter We even used to end up putting on the stereo and dancing, usually jiving, what great times they really were. She even persuaded me to join the local Beaumont society, which is a society known nationally for cross dressers and transvestites. Wives are more than welcome and so she came along as well, she was welcomed with open arms by all who attended, for her support to me, as not every wife accepts it. She became well sought after for her opinion for their clothes and any other tips she offered. We even went to various balls and events which were laid on by the society, which in turn helped me no end, not only by going out dressed, but with my own acceptance of my cross dressing. I remember well coming home one evening after attending one such event, parking the car near as I could to our flat, then whilst walking the short distance to our back door, being approached by a group of young lads, and asked" are you two doing business?"

After nearly dying on the spot, my immediate reaction was to run as fast as my shaky legs would carry me, leaving my wife to be with this very amorous group of lads. Unlike me she decided to stay there and wind them right up, and only leaving them with these parting words "you are only boys with boys money, come back when you are men with a mans wallet". How she thought that one up god only knows, never the less she walked away leaving them gagging at the mouth trying to raise as much cash as they could between them. Then as she got around the corner, ran like hell to our back door and burst in with fits of laughter calling me a coward bitch for leaving her to talk her way out of it. I think it must have been a good hour before we both stopped laughing enough to reflect on the evening's excitement. But excitement it was and the fear of being caught out was also a huge thrill for both of us, and like me she was also very inquisitive to the comings and goings of theses so called ladies of the night and equally as amazed at what they were earning and the speed they were doing it in, especially with the fact that they were not very attractive. I think that this evening's escapade set seeds in both our heads.

After a few months had passed, and my female side had really progressed, I mentioned to my partner that, I wished I could have found someone like her many years sooner than I did. How I had scoured the ads in various papers to try and find a one to one service with a woman who understood my needs. Who could also advise me on what to wear, how to apply make up, and to go shopping with me [me being in male mode] to purchase all the things I needed for my femme creation. She was amazed when I told her that I never found anyone for that purpose, especially given the fact that her own experience with some of the members of the Beaumont society asking for the same type of service. As a result she suggested that we should place an ad in a paper and offer a dressing service for the closet transvestites, after all she was a very fashionable lady who loves dressing up and of course shopping, so nothing ventured nothing gained we, duly placed an ad. The response was quite surprising and soon had our first customer, but of course overlooked by us, was the question asked by most of the customers. "Are there any extras to the service?" We were quite naïve and inquired what they actually wanted. It appeared that most of them wanted some kind of domination role-play, I suppose I could associate with these needs, and as when I am dressed I too feel submissive. So my partner and I discussed various role-play games to offer them. After explaining to her the domme role for her to perform, she was more than happy to accommodate. Well most women like to get their own way and have the upper hand, so she was well away with that role. As I was of the submissive nature I could guide her as and when required, we performed as a duo very well and bounced off each other during our little games with the clients. As time passed we learnt our profession well, and although every one was different, most of the games were of similar nature, but all with the same end result of satisfaction for the clients. If the truth were told most of the time we found it interesting and enjoyable as well.

After a couple of years or so my wife suggested that I should place an ad for Susie on her own as a tv escort. I dismissed this straight away, saying that " I don't think that there would be enough call for that" especially as our present ad already offered singles or duo, and we didn't get much response for me on my own. So that idea was put on the back burner, never the less not long after the suggestion was made we did start to get a few calls for me on my own, which rather surprised me, and if I speak the truth excited me as well. After taking the first booking for Susie on her own I started to wonder if it was a good idea after all, thankfully for me my first client as a single was a proper tv admirer who wanted to be completely dominated, and controlled by me. I found this easy to do as it was right up my street. The client was most impressed by not only my appearance, but also my confident services and ability to perform my role as his mistress to his complete satisfaction, so much so that he has become one of my regulars still to this very day. It was really funny for me to come out of the bedroom after his session and shout downstairs to my waiting wife "pop the kettle on darling for two coffees", [a role that I had done for her on many occasions]. We both laughed at that afterwards, but to me that felt great not only as a competent escort, but as the breadwinner again.

As time went by I started to get more and more single bookings for Susie and my confidence grew with each job. I always had my wife assisting me with the meeting and greeting along with initial chat, and of course she always stayed in the house whilst Susie was doing her work with the client, which in turn obviously gave me great comfort.

I suppose the thing that concerned me more than anything was the thought of getting one of those extreme clients that we as a couple had performed with in the past. Which had been an eye opener to say the least. Some people would say that they are weird, and indeed so did I in the past, but after 9 years or so performing as an escort, I have reached the conclusion that there is no such thing as normal. Every one has there own form of fetishism in one form or another. Quite honestly I never yet had two the same, very similar but not exactly the same. Whilst I was not concerned for safety reasons, being more than capable to take care of myself, I was more concerned about bursting in fits of laughter at some strange request, and believe me there have been many of those, as you will find out in the following chapters. Fortunately for me my first client on my own was to say the least a pussycat.

During the next year or so, our private entertaining had to take a back seat, for my business was engaged in a development project, which needed my full attention. As managing director I had negotiated a loan of 225 thousand pounds to build three houses on some land which I owned personally. As the loan had a built in repayment scheme for the first 12 months, it was in my interest to get them built as soon as possible, and preferably sold within the year. We agreed that I would work from dawn to dusk 7 days pr week until they were ready to sell. To keep the costs down I would do as much of the work as I was able, and employ as few as possible. A huge burden for me with a lot of worry attached, and for someone who has had 2 heart attacks, along with a mild stroke, was probably too much to take on. Never the less I accepted the challenge and met it head on, looking back I don't think that my wife realised just what was involved, and the sacrifices we would have to make as a couple.

There would be no holidays, no breaks, and no let up until complete, so the advert for our escorting business would have to come out, as

I would not have the time for entertaining, and if she were going to help neither would she, but the rewards were worth it. After all I am a firm believer in the saying' you only get out what you put in'. Whilst she started with the best of intentions her enthusiasm and devotion for the project came in fits and starts. She started taking the odd two-week break to visit relatives on her own. Leaving me on my own to run the business as well as look after the house with the 2 dogs, along with cooking my meals and general household duties all of which added to my pressures. Still as luck would have it even though we had the wettest year on record, I completed my task, and was fortunate enough to sell one house off plan, after only getting the foundations completed. The second house was sold for the full asking price once completed, this paid off the bank in full, [first hurdle out of the way] all within the 12 month period. Now to finish off the last one, where all my wages and profit lay. True to form as I was finishing off the last house my luck ran out, along came the credit crunch and still to this very day some 3 years after completing the house I still have not sold that property. In stead I have rented it out until times are better, so I still have not yet had my wages or profit for that year of hardship, ah well one day perhaps.

Because I had been successful in my endeavours with paying the bank off within the 12 months, they encouraged me to take out another loan. There was an old large house with some land attached, which stood right behind my recent project and had been empty since moving into the area. I opened up negotiations with the current owner to purchase it for re development into a large block of apartments, [4 in all]. Splitting the remaining land into car parking for the flats, which would leave me enough land for a further pair of semi- detached houses to develop at a later date, or sell on as prime building plots to another developer. So off I went again, another 12 months hard graft, along with another year of no entertaining fun, although there was a period of approximately 3 months whilst waiting for planning permission when we re advertised our little business. I must admit it felt good to be back again especially as all those hard long hours were getting to me and taking their toll. I think that I knew there and then where my remaining years of work lay, not as a builder but as a tv escort providing that I could get enough clients to make it worth while financially, only time will tell after all nothing ventured nothing gained. That's always been my motto so why change now. As time went by we eventually got our planning permission, and so it was back on the tools again. By now my wife was becoming more and more homesick, and just as I was starting back working on site, 4 weeks before Christmas she decided over night to leave me and go back to her homeland.

I think this was one of the biggest blows to me since losing my father many years ago. I really thought that she was my proper soul mate who would stand by me through thick and thin. After all it was her that had brought the femme side of me out of the darkness of the closet and had really enjoyed working with me in our little business and shared all the laughs that went with the job. She had always told me that she was very proud of her creation in Susie and would always be there for her. This contract was to be the last before retiring to a better life. With the expected profits from the eventual sales of the properties we were going to do lots more travel to European countries on the Mediterranean coast in our own small live aboard boat, taking in as many inland canal routes as possible. Only returning to the U. K. for about 4 months per year to keep in touch with friends and family. We had even planned to sell our large 4 bed detached house and down size to a more modest 2 bed home. It seemed unwise to tie up a lot of capital in a house so large, which we were only going to live in for a few weeks per year. For when the day comes to stop our travelling and stay home for good, we certainly didn't need such a large house to run and maintain. So after many years of planning and talking every aspect of our future through and through, to suddenly find that the rug has been pulled from beneath me was to say the least a shattering blow.

That Christmas was to me one of the worst ones I have ever had, and still to this very day I look upon that time of the year with sadness in my heart and I am always glad when the New Year is well and truly behind me. It's a shame really because as a small boy, like all kids

I had some very memorable Christmases with my family, but never since have been repeated, its true Christmas is for kids and that's how it should stay, but I am afraid us men never properly grow up. Still that first festive season on my own again, gave me the opportunity to think about my future in great detail. Keeping in mind that there is always someone worse off than yourself I came to the conclusion that the plans that we as a couple had made were good ones and just because I was now on my own saw no good reason to change them.

After all, I have come so far to achieving that goal why walk away from it now. I have already started my last contract, I have the means to carry on with my escorting business, and I have the perfect house to enable me to do so. My ex wife had really done a good job in creating Susie, which in turn gave me the confidence to blossom in my new role as a transvestite escort. With all those clothes, wigs, and shoes that had been so carefully bought for her, its about time they earned there keep. So I changed the advert in the local weekly paper from the duo act, to just myself, a convincing, attractive sexy, transvestite offering a full dressing service with massage, in luxury surroundings, discrete, and unhurried. I bought a new mobile phone with a new number, and just waited for the ad to come out and see what happens. Well what a surprise my phone never stopped ringing, taking about 25 to 30 calls per day, most of which I hasten to add were timewasters, still I managed to do about 1 job per day, usually in the evening as I was still working by day building my block of 4 apartments. At weekends I could sometimes do 2 jobs per day, especially if it was raining, its funny but the rain seems to make the clients more aware of my services than sunshine. Never the less I was overwhelmed by the response to my advert, and completely taken by surprise I would never have thought that there were so many men who wanted that kind of service, but there you go, there is nowt so queer as folk [pardon the pun]. This only convinced me even more that I was doing the right thing. I am not one of those kind of person that dwells in the past, throw yourself into your work and get on with it, that I find is my best way of getting through difficult times, and that's just what I needed right now.

The balance of hard work on site as Peter, and the fun work indoors as Susie made time go by rather quickly. Before I knew where I was spring was upon me, in the meantime I had lost 2 stone in weight through not having time to cook proper meals for myself, little sleep, and lots of work. Still that's just what Susie needed, down to size 12 some of my skirts were even size 10, the trouble was not many of my existing clothes fitted me now, so I had to buy some new ones. How the hell am I going to do that I thought to myself, after all my ex wife did all the buying in the past, she is not here now so I will have to do it. Then I remembered that I have an account with a shopping catalogue, easy, problem solved. Now I know just how you women feel when shopping bloody marvellous what a therapy, I am sorry for you men, but you will never understand just how us girls feel when buying new clothes, I am hooked.

I think that my main concern of going solo as an escort was what if I got one of those really way out clients with a strange request, like some of the ones we attracted as a duo. At least then we always had each other to bounce off when the situation was getting a little stagnant, but looking back now there was no need to have worried, nothing has ever come my way that I didn't handle. Before I embarked into this world of escorting I used to think that there were a lot of weird people out there, but now that I am well established after 8 years or so of experience, I have come to the conclusion that there is no such thing as normal. Every body is different, some more extreme than others but on the whole all very harmless, and in the next few chapters I will tell you of some of the varying role plays that I have encountered. All of which I hasten to add were performed with the greatest professionalism to complete satisfaction, resulting in many a return visit for repeat experiences. However I do lay down certain ground rules, no drugs of any type, the game stops immediately when either party says the safety word. This is a word pre-arranged by both of us before the game starts, usually orange. No hard sports, no cutting/ bleeding of any kind and the ending of all games is left to my discretion.

Where couples are concerned married or not, I will need to talk to the female on her own in private, before any action starts to make sure that she is in full agreement of the situation. So any men have these fantasies in their heads, and sometimes try to force the partner into their little games without prior full consultation.

Believe me quite a few couples do contact me to fulfil their fantasies, usually when their sex life is on the wane and need a little something to spice up there fun times.

Now all you men reading this might think; lucky bugger; but trust me its not always as good as you think, especially when you have 2 people of opposite sex to please at the same time. You need to put on an act that you are also enjoying the same experience, remember you cant say no when they are paying for your performance, [thank god for Viagra]. I now know how you girls feel when having to fake your orgasm, and have learnt the art extremely well. The things us girls have to do, just remember all you guys the next time you make love to your partner, and she makes all the right noises, at all the right times, did she really climax or was it a very good act? You think you know, but only she knows for sure, I wonder how many of you ladies out there who may be reading this book have now got a smile on there faces, umm me too.

Its funny but whilst dressed as Susie women seem to warm to me, I think it is because they feel safe with me as a woman. I do really love the girly conversations we may have, they have helped me to understand a woman's way of thinking, but never totally, like most of you men I still get baffled now and again.

Chapter 9
THE HANGMAN

I suppose the title sounds a little intimidating but rest assured it's not as bad as it sounds, and bear in mind that all of the role play games are carefully planned out and rehearsed for everybody's complete safety, long before the actual games commence. We first encountered Terry, a successful industrialist from the Southeast of England through our national advert whilst living in the Northeast. He was intrigued by our role-play and wanted to know more. Terry lived in London and often travelled the length and breadth of the U.K. with his job. He didn't want to say too much over the phone, instead made an appointment to visit us the next time that he was in the area, where he could discuss his fantasy face to face.

The day duly arrived for his visit, and we were both anxious to hear of his secretive fantasy request, to say that we were shocked when listening to his strange request would be an understatement, nevertheless after thorough discussions with my wife it was agreed to give it a try. After all it was going to take place in our own home, under our rules, and more importantly under our supervision.

Terry certainly did have a strange fantasy; he was obsessed with olden day's public hangings, and all the rigmarole that goes with it, including the court case leading up to the execution, with him being the judge, jailer, and executioner. He even had books and manuscripts on actual events which had taken place many years ago, both in this country and abroad, along with various props and period clothing, for both him and the accused. He also had obtained various video tapes of similar such events for us to watch, and learn from them to fulfil his fantasy to the maximum. Most of the recordings were of poor quality, mostly foreign pornography involving bondage and sadomasochism, so obviously that was his fetish, just a weird strain of it. I suppose he loved to have the power over his subjects, the more the power the more the thrill.

The first part of the game was to watch a film of the actual court case and take note of the victim's reaction to the verdict and how it was reached. In the meantime I had set up a courtroom scene in our large living room, by removing most of the furniture, then setting up a makeshift judges bench, by draping a black sheet over the dining table and placing a large high backed chair behind it. Then by laying the kitchen table on its side and placing high backed chairs behind and to one side of this table formed the dock in which stood the accused. A small wooden box was placed on the floor behind it for my partner to stand on, making her feel vulnerable. I stood to one side of her acting as her jailer and court usher, leading her to the dock for the hearing, and away afterwards back to her so called cell whilst waiting for the courts verdict, then back again for sentencing. What a bloody rigmarole this was turning out to be, I felt like Mr shifter on that PG tips advert, I thought if this doesn't work out I could always get a job with Pickford's furniture removals. As you can tell my wife and I did not take this little game too seriously. In fact we were trying hard to keep straight faces whilst all this was going on, especially when confronted with Terry's face who was taking everything so seriously. The more involved he became the more strange expressions he would portray on his face. Fortunately for my wife she had to hold her head low for the whole of the so called court case, so she could not see his facial expressions, where as I was looking straight at him. I could see all of his weird twisted looks whilst at the same time sticking his tongue out, how I never burst out in fits of laughter I shall never know. I happened to tell my wife later, whatever you do never look up to see his face, if so I am sure you will wet yourself with laughter. During all of this role play I was obviously dressed in male mode, occasionally having to change my clothes from usher to jailer, and so on, as well as having to change the props and scenery. During these times they would take a tea break, whilst going over the lines for the next part of the game. He really did take it all very seriously and paid special attention to every little detail, he had even highlighted certain lines on the script, which needed emphasising. He would make us both go over and over again until he was sure that we were saying it correctly, [very difficult to do and still keep a straight face]. When the props and scenery were ready for the grand finale, we would have a couple of minutes to get our composure correct and then walk through into the large living room to play our parts. Now to set the scene for you what I had to do in the preparation for this grand finale was to set up the execution scene. I would have formed a hangman's noose into a white thick rope, then taped it to the ceilings so that it was hanging down with the noose at head height for my wife, [I must have gone through a whole roll of tape trying to make that bloody rope stick to my ceiling]. It was all perfectly safe, the rope hardly held itself let alone the weight of a person. I would place a large white sheet on the wood block floor underneath the rope, then in front of this scene place a large box on the floor for him to stand on whilst he read out the sentence of death by hanging. For this scene my wife would be dressed in a white robe, and I would be dressed in an executioners black cloak with hood. Terry also would be dressed in a black cloak with the customary black cap. He would be in the room first, and I would have to lead the prisoner from the condemned cell, into this room ready for execution, [we would always make him wait a few minutes before entering]. This gave us time to compose ourselves and try to get a straight face, as we were both trying hard not to laugh, because we knew that by now he would be pulling the most funniest of faces. Oh yes and his tongue would be sticking right out by now, but the funniest thing would be the fact that he would be masturbating himself furiously. Now you try and keep a straight face whilst that lots going on, there was also a good reason for lots of tea drinking as you will soon know. Well I would knock three times on the door and wait for him to announce enter, [like something from black rod at the house of parliament]. I would then lead the prisoner in and take her to the awaiting noose, by now she would be crying and begging for her life and mercy. He would be reading out her sentence and last rites, with momentarily pauses for his by now, fierce periods of masturbation. Timing was of the essence here, because once he had climaxed that was the end of the game, so it was up to me to roughly know when that would be. The only inclination I would have would be the facial expressions, but there was my dilemma, for when I looked at his face all twisted with a tongue sticking out I just wanted to laugh, thank god I had a hood on to hide my smirking face. He did however give me some clues to when that might be by telling me when to place the rope around her neck, and in turn my wife would plead all the more at this request, all of which would heighten his pleasure. The major part of my wife's role now was to urinate she as the rope was placed around her neck, hence the white sheet on the floor, and all the tea drinking. This was usually done when he had reached the part where he says "may God have mercy on your wicked soul". This always did the trick, and he would always climax at this point thank god.

Afterwards we would all get changed back into our normal clothes, go into the drawing room and have an inquest about the last hour or so over another cup of tea. He would tell us which parts he enjoyed the best which parts we should emphasise on, and the parts of the plot we could improve on for his next visit.

Altogether we saw Terry 4 times, he wanted to come back on several occasions, but my wife and I had talked in great depths about his fetish and we decided that we did not want to get involved with him again. I am sure you will agree that the thought of such a severe fetish seemed a little disturbing to say the least, especially as each time he came it seemed to get more and more severe, and we did not want to know where it would all end.

Just one footnote I will add, and that is on his last visit my wife had her back to him at one point of the game, and unbeknown to her she lifted her head and could see his face in the mirror nearly on the point of his climax. She burst out in uncontrollable laughter, giving the excuse that she had just remembered a really funny joke and could not get it out of her head, we all had to take 5 just to regain our composure, [I did tell her not to look!!!]

Since our last encounter with Terry, I have made many friends through on line sites for the transvestite scene, and as a result met some very interesting friends. Through a friend of a friend Terry's name and fetish came up in conversation, and I was told some very disturbing news of him and so looking back the right decision was made to putting an end to his visits.

Thankfully he was one of a kind, and I have never encountered any one like him since. As the years have past I have learnt to categorise peoples role-play and fantasies during their initial phone call, and steered well clear of any of the strong sadomasochism clients. That's not to say I don't enjoy being the dominatrix, that's fine I am in complete control and fortunately most of my clients require just that as you will see when reading on.

Chapter 10
LITTLE BO PEEP

Not all of my work comes from the area weekly paper, and as a sign of the modern times I have finally succumbed to the twenty first century by getting myself a computer, every one told me its easy [bloody liars]. I have lost count of how many times my computer has nearly had a flying lesson through my office window amidst very blue air filled with lots of varying four lettered words. Never the less I have pursued and nearly conquered the art using one. I say nearly because I only use one when I have to, and I know my limitations, as long as I stay to doing just what I know there is no problem. I must admit I have found them very helpful in joining transvestite sites and making some very good likeminded friends world wide, and have had many visits from other transvestites, not just from this country, but also from overseas. You really would be surprised just how many cross dressers there are in this world, and all of them feel unique and some of them very lonely. Statistics tell us that 3 out of 5 men are cross dressers of one form or another, how true that is I don't know, but I will say that I have been really surprised by the amount of contacts I have made through these sites. In fact nearly fifty percent of my work now comes via the Internet. One such client [for privacy sake I will call him Tony] made contact with me via the Internet and after several subsequent phone calls made an appointment to visit me. As with all clients upon his arrival the first thirty minutes or so is spent seated in the drawing room having a good heart to heart chat discussing his requirements over a good old fashioned cup of tea. Once both parties are comfortable with each other off we go upstairs to the playroom for the fun to begin.

Well Tony who incidentally is a university lecturer of high standing likes to be dominated and trained as a maid whilst dressed as a sissy Bo peep, a role which I adapt to very well. He also told me that he likes to be punished and spanked as hard as I think fit during his learning curve. Although this is not an uncommon request I have found in the past that most of the thrill of this type of game is all in the head, and as soon as the punishment starts and reality kicks in the mental fascination is overtaken by the physical pain and the safety word soon appears. Its always difficult to know how far to go on the first appointment, therefore it's a gentle build up until signs of the safety word then pull back into an enjoyable zone and stay within those limits.

After our chat over a cup of tea Tony asked me if he could go upstairs to prepare and change into his uniform which he had brought with him.

When he was ready he would come back downstairs knock the drawing room door and wait for instructions. So after showing him to the spare en suite room, I then retired back to the drawing room with another cup of tea and a cigarette and duly waited for the knock. It must have been at least an hour that had gone by with no sight or sound of my sissy maid, and I was beginning to think that he had either bottled out, or was in need of assistance. I shouted up the stairs "are you ok up there?""Oh yes" came the very feeble reply " I won't be long now". After about another 20 minutes or so came that knock, knock on my door," Come in" I said. The door opened slowly and there stood what I can only describe as a little Bo peep. She stood there in white satin flat shoes, white ankle socks, over white silk stockings, a blue satin dress with lots and lots of petticoats which made the dress flare out. Little white gloves, and a white maids apron completed the outfit. She wore heavy make up, which had been put on immaculately, along with a pretty white bow in her black bob wig. She presented herself to me with a curtsey, then placed her hands by her side and lowered her head, she really did look the part and I could now see why she had taken so long in her preparation it was meticulous for her roll as my sissy maid. Your first chore is to make me another pot of tea whilst I decide what punishment to administer for keeping me waiting. " Yes mistress" came the very feeble reply, as she was now into her role proper. When she had returned with my refreshments which were presented to me on a silver tray along with another curtsey, I told her that after I had drunk my tea I will be inspecting her thoroughly and that anything found that does not meet my standards will be punished severely. This seemed to excite her immensely, I was dressed in a smart black suit, with matching shoes and stockings, and a white silk top, I always found that black was a strong colour perfect for a domination role.

I slowly drank my tea whilst she stood motionless before me with head lowered, and in between my sips, remarked on how much of a sissy she really did look, and that the mere sight of her made me want to punish her. "Yes mistress I am so sorry" came her repeated reply. "You will be after I have inspected you" I told her. This really struck the right notes, as by now she was shaking with excitement.

I did not make her wait too long before standing in front of her whilst scrutinising her appearance. I lifted her dress to display white silky French knickers along with a blue garter and blue suspender belt and lo and behold one of the stocking stays had come undone. "Upstairs now to the punishment room" I exclaimed, "follow me"."Yes mistress" she squeaked. I lead and she followed me to my bedroom [in this case the punishment room]. Once there I informed her to raise her dress, pull down her knickers to her knees, bend over my bed, and wait for her punishment. She did this immediately with a pleasing " yes mistress". I then slapped each cheek several times until they were glowing red. She really did enjoy this humiliating punishment, and even replied "do you think I have been punished enough mistress?" "Not yet" I said sensing that she could take a lot more than that. "You realise that your pain is my pleasure don't you?" I asked. She excitedly replied "in that case mistress you must give me as much pain as you wish". This was her way of telling me that she was enjoying what I was doing and could go much further. With that understood I ordered her to lay face down on my bed, spread eagled with her arms wide apart, restraining each wrist to a bedpost with leather straps and chains, then with leather ankle straps and chains did the same to her legs. Her French knickers were by now stretched wide apart to the point of ripping but still around her knees, and the dress was pulled up even further, exposing a rosy pair of eagerly waiting cheeks. Over the years I have acquired quite a collection of punishment tools. Several whips, paddles, riding crops and canes, along with leather straps and clusters of birch branches, all of which were laid out beside her on the bed near her face for her to see. I then lit several candles which I placed around the room, turned off the main lights, all of which set the scene with the right ambience for what was to come.

"Now" I sternly exclaimed "I am going to enjoy myself, and you must always remember that your pain is my pleasure and I want lots. As you are well and truly tied down with no freedom in your chain restraints there is absolutely nothing you can do to stop me". "No mistress I wouldn't dream of stopping your pleasure" came her reply bear in mind that there was a safety word available and I would of course stopped immediately if the word was mentioned. Starting with a nice leather strap I duly gave her several strokes with a belt on each cheek." Now let me try one of my paddles" that really did crack out, six on each cheek, which were getting redder by the second. To my surprise she never flinched let alone mentions the safety word. Christ I thought she can take it, so I reached over and picked up one of my whips, a small cat o nine tails made from soft leather, but still effective. She shook with excitement at the anticipation of receiving several lashes of the whip, at the same time I was dishing out lots of verbal abuse to her calling her a useless sissy slut, all of which heightened her pleasure. I started off with light strokes and gradually built up to more severe lashes, but the harder they came the more she seemed to enjoy it. Believe me they must have hurt, so I stopped for a few minutes after several lashes and poured some baby lotion on her well and truly marked cheeks, gently rubbing in the cream to soothe the red hot cheeks, but never letting up on the verbal remarks. To say she was in ecstasy was an understatement, good God I thought I don't know about her arse but my arm was starting to ache, how much more will she take? To test the water I said, " I am really getting lots of pleasure now" " oh good mistress I aim to please you" came the reply, so with no sign of a let up I continued. "Well lets use the riding crop, this makes a nice whishing noise as it comes down" I said" then I will finish off with the canes, that will make you sorry for not pleasing me with your poorly arranged suspender belt". "Please continue mistress," she said. Well there was no more starting off light I went straight in with half a dozen hard strokes on each cheek. To my surprise there was not a flinch. I then poured hot candle wax straight over the welts and still no reaction, so after the wax had set on her reddened marked cheeks I picked up the bamboo cane and laid straight into the punishing strokes. Now this did create a reaction she started jumping up and down as much as she could under the restraints, but still no sign of the safety word being mentioned. So I got some cheap after shave lotion and poured some of that on the welts which were at the point of breaking, although this made her take in large gulps of breath, it still kept the safety word silent.

By now my arms were well and truly aching after 2 hours of punishment and I wasn't prepared to go any further on this our first appointment. I certainly did not want to go over the top and put her off from a return visit, so I told her that she had received all the punishment she was going to get this evening. She was to get changed back into male mode and come downstairs for some refreshments before her long journey home. As it was now well after midnight and we both would have work to go to tomorrow, we could continue this game on another occasion. She readily agreed to my request, and after getting changed joined me downstairs with a nightcap of a single malt whisky. We sat and chatted for a while, whereupon he [as by now the female side was completely gone] told me that he had really enjoyed himself and would certainly be coming back for further encounters of the same.

After he had gone I thought to myself that must have hurt especially having to sit down on that backside for that long journey back to his home. To my disbelief, the very next day I received a text message from him saying that he had really enjoyed himself, and that he couldn't wait to pay me another visit for more of the same, but could I please give him much harder strokes next time. He has paid me several visits since that first encounter and it took me three appointments before I made him say the safety word. Once reached I never took him that far again, for its best to find the limits and then stay just below them for maximum effect and pleasure.

Chapter 11
THE P.E. POLITICIAN

Now for the sake of privacy and anonymity I will give him the name of Harry, although I will only mention that he is a politician. There will be no mention of what party he represents, or any indication of his location and position he holds, except to say that he is frequently interviewed on the television for his views on varying subjects, and no more than that will I ever reveal.

Although Harry has only ever paid me two visits to date they certainly left an impression on me. He has tried to make several appointments since his last visit, but on all dates given to me, I was previously pre booked or not available at those times, so no doubt Harry will be trying again in the near future.

Peter Edwards

It must be over a year ago when Harry first phoned me to enquire about the services provided. I say first, because like most of my clients they usually make several phone calls asking all sorts of questions before plucking up the courage to make a confirmed booking. The thing which intrigued him more than anything was the fact that I have the wardrobe and ability to offer more or less any kind of scenario [within reason] that he wanted. So he wanted to leave the final choice until his arrival, and even then wanted to know if I could change half way through into a different role with appropriate clothing to suit. No problem, he who pays the piper calls the tune, and as far as I am concerned a change is as good as a rest. The appointment was made and on the day in question he promptly knocked my door to the minute of the agreed time, and as usual Susie dressed to the nines in a smart tart short suit said "oh please come in darling".

In came Harry a smart gentleman in his late fifties, early sixties carrying a bottle of wine along with a plain white envelope. "The wine is for us to drink now darling, and the envelope contains the agreed fee, I thought that we would get that out of the way first then we can enjoy ourselves darling, ok?" "Oh yes thank you kind sir" I answered, thinking to myself I wont count it out now he looks the type to trust, and I certainly did not want to offend him by doing so. We sat in the drawing room and I opened the wine then started to talk about his fantasies and what sort of scenario he would like to day. Well he also was like a kid in a sweet shop with all different kinds of role plays he was into, so I suggested two differing games we could play, and as time was of the essence this would be all we can do in the time given to day. He agreed and then went into great depths of his first choice, which was, for me to be a shop assistant who worked in a large department store, and he was employed as the stores health adviser. As he was an ex doctor he will be giving me a check over to make sure that I was in first class condition as well as giving me a proper examination it was also his responsibility to ensure that I had a 100% physical stamina ability. Good god I thought what the hell is he going to do, too bloody late now he has paid me I have got to go through with it.

As I was already dressed as a smart tart it was agreed that I could stay in this uniform for the first part of the game, in the meantime Harry went back to his car to fetch a few props that he had brought with him. When he returned I went into the dining room and re arranged the dining table to form a kind of shop counter. I then went to the clothes room brought a few clothes down and placed them on the table, stood behind it as if it were a counter then started to fold the clothes up to make myself look busy like an assistant would do. I was now in character, then in walks Harry and presents himself to me announcing that he was the stores doctor and that he wanted to give me a private consultation to check my health.

To do this I was to follow him to his private room [my bedroom] where he would be able to do this right now especially as I am not too busy at present, [well I wouldn't be would I, no bugger would be coming into my dining room to buy any clothes]. So off we both went, once we arrived in the bedroom Harry went in his little bag of props and pulled out a stethoscope, and a thermometer. " Pop this under your tongue whilst I listen to your heart and feel your pulse". "Yes doctor" I replied thinking once again what the bloody hell am doing, at the same time trying not to laugh and keep in character. I must admit when looking at him doing is doctor bit how realistic he looked. Then whilst listening at my heartbeat he did that sort of frown that doctors often do, CHRIST I hope he hasn't found anything wrong [flashed through my head] but no it was just part of the act. "How many miles a day do you walk?" he asked. " Oh let me see it must be at least 3", I said. "THREE" he shouted" nothing like enough, you must walk at least 8 every day". Good god I thought that would bloody kill me, if I have to go to the local shop 200yds away I will take the car. "Umm" he muttered "I had better give you some exercises to do whilst I monitor your condition".

Now it was from this point onwards that I really had to fight back the laughter fits, he then went into the en-suite bathroom with his little bag of tricks and came out a few seconds later dressed as I can only describe like my old p.e. teacher at school. He stood there in white plimsolls, blue socks, blue shorts, and a white vest, along with a whistle hung around his neck by a red and blue ribbon. "Right young lady strip down to your underwear, leaving on your stockings and shoes, then come and stand in front of me and follow my actions". Well I do not like getting undressed down to my underwear whilst I am dressed as a women for obvious reasons like not having a real pair of breasts, and of course having a large bulge in the front of my panties. But I do have to go through with it now there is no turning back, so off it all came, well just the skirt, jacket and top. "My my he said you do have a large clitoris Miss Susie don't you?" [How I stopped myself from pissing my pants with laughter I shall never know] but I managed to contain myself. Then he started to do some exercises by jumping up in the air clapping his hands over his head, and at the same time alternating his legs from apart to together. Well when I started to do this in unison with him the bedroom floor literally bounced making one hell of a thud. So much so that the two dogs I own who were lying downstairs must have thought that we were being invaded by a herd of wild buffalo, and started a frenzied bark, convinced that the ceiling was going to collapse on top of them with us two silly buggers dressed for p.e. along with it. Then to top it all off he blew his sodding whistle, this only created even more havoc to the two canines below, who by now were howling the death howl in-between their barking whilst running around in circles.

"Stop" he shouted. "Every time I blow this whistle it means we change the exercise". He was obviously deaf to all the havoc he had created below him, "now" he said "this new exercise is as follows, legs apart, and swing your arms from up in the air to touching your toes, first right hand to left toe then left hand to right toe". He blew his f***ing whistle again to mark the start of the exercise, the dogs went scatty again the poor buggers I don't have a clue what must have been going through their heads, but I know what was going through mine. If any body could see me now I would be certified, especially as one of my false breasts had fallen out with all this f***ing jumping about, and I was trying to kick it under the bed out of sight. As this particular exercise was relatively quiet, the dogs had gone reasonably silent, that is until [you have guessed it] the silly twat blew that pissing whistle again, and shouted "STOP". " Now Miss Susie I will bet that your leg muscles are stiffening up after all this exercise aren't they?" With that he started to rub his hands up and down my legs front, back, and sides, very slowly making sure that he felt every inch of silky nylon clad legs.

Ah I thought this must be where he gets his thrill, because the last quarter of an hour has not been very exciting. What with the declaration of war going on down stairs, and me gasping for breath with all my arm and leg muscles aching as if I had just run the marathon, and him blowing that f***ing whistle, I had just about come to the end of my tether.

After about 10 minutes of Harry stroking my whole body, with me standing still before him, he said "right I think we will take a 5 minute break now, have another glass of wine each, then you can get changed in preparation for the next scenario". "Good idea" I said," it will give me a chance to pop down stairs and give the dogs some Valium". He did not see the funny side, I think he was oblivious to all the pandemonium going on below him.

During our wine break, Harry talked about the second part of the role-play, in which he wanted me to dress as a school head mistress and he was going to be a naughty schoolboy. No problem for me as I do have a teachers uniform with mortar board hat and all, along with a teachers cane [very important piece of equipment] as a lot of my clients like the school teachers scenario, as well as my raunchy St Trinians outfit. The theme was to be on the lines as follows. He as a schoolboy had been into some kind of mischief in class and as a result had been sent to me to reprimand him. Whilst being left alone in my study [bedroom] to wait for my arrival, could not resist looking through my belongings and finding a pair of my knickers. At that point I was to enter the room and catch him in the act, resulting in me making him wear them to receive his punishment. Easy one I thought, at least we haven't got that bloody whistle,

By now the little bag of tricks that he had brought with him was empty, so he kept on his existing clothes just adding a jacket, and I let him have a schoolboys cap just to add to the feel of the scene. With our wine finished we went back upstairs [leaving the dogs spaced out on tranquillisers] and I sent Harry into the bedroom to wait for me whilst I got changed, brushed my hair, and freshened up my make up. When I eventually entered the room Harry was looking very sheepish standing by my chest of drawers. "What are you doing there Harry?" I sternly said. "Nothing miss", he replied. "Let me see, turn around" and as he did so he revealed a pair of my panties sticking out of his pocket. "What are you doing with those?" I asked. " Nothing miss", "don't lie to me boy what are you doing?" " Well I wanted to take them back to my dorm miss". "WHY?" I enquired. "Well miss I was going to wear them when I go to bed tonight and sleep in them all night". "Oh I see you want to wear ladies knickers do you?" "Only yours miss", came the sultry reply. "Well you put them on now in front of me then". "Yes miss" he squeaked, and as soon as he had stretched them over his naked buttocks and cock he immediately got an erection. "Stand there boy, and let me see how ridiculous you look". Harry stood to attention with arms by his side straight as a die, and so was his cock. "Now boy bend over and touch your toes", "what over your knee miss?" Taking this as a request more than an inquiry, I said, "yes to start with. I wont be able to punish you with the cane at such close quarters over my knee, so I will start with my hand, then whilst stood alone touching your toes will give you six of the best. The first punishment is for being sent here in the first place, and the six with the cane for stealing my panties". As he lay over my knees my teachers cloak which is split from top to bottom at the front fell to one side revealing my stocking clad legs all the way to the top of my thighs. As he lay his naked body [apart from the knickers he was wearing] across my legs I could feel him rubbing his manhood over the top of my legs getting more and more excited. I spanked him good and hard, remembering all that jumping and whistle blowing he had put me through and started to get my own back. Then before I could get him to stand, I felt the rubbing of his body against my thighs getting faster and faster, coupled with sharp intakes of breath, knowing that the end was not that far away. I started to call him a very very naughty boy, who because of his misdemeanours will have to wear my knickers 24hrs per day for the next whole week. This soon did the trick before long I felt the warm wetness on my knees, together with the mutterings of ooh, ooh, and ooh. I pushed him off my knees, as with all that bloody jumping around and his weight on them for the last ten minutes or so they really were aching. Noticing that not only were my knickers which he was wearing were wet, but so were my stockings." Look at these stockings "I told him. "You have got to take them home with you and wash them by hand not in a machine along with those panties and bring them back with you next time, is that understood?" "Oh certainly miss". I never did get them back, but I knew that when I told him to take them.

After he had got showered, changed, and left my house, I sat in the living room thinking back on the afternoons charade and whilst reassuring my 2 dogs that all was well in the household, burst out laughing at the whole episode. I should get an award for my acting skills I thought, what a way to try and earn a living, but compared with standing on a cold windy scaffold laying bricks in the rain, I know what I would rather do.

Chapter 12
THE COUPLE

You may think it strange to think those married [or otherwise] couples

would need the services of a transvestite escort, but believe me it is quite common to get enquiries for that service What kind of service you may be asking, well

The first type is the couple who has talked between themselves about the wife having a sexual fling with another woman. It has always been a turn on for most men to see two women together, especialy if one of them happens to be his wife. In reality this could be disastrous especially if the wife found out that she prefers women to men. The husband/

male partner could find that he has lost his partner to a woman, and he is not involved in the relationship thereafter. Where as with a convincing transvestite he doesn't feel so threatened. As for the wife, she feels safer with the [half way house transvestite] knowing that although she is seeing a woman, in reality it's a man, and she can experiment without emotions getting in the way. All resulting in an evening's fun all round with no permanent damage afterwards for either partner.

Secondly its basically the same but in reverse, where as the woman would like to se her male partner with another woman, but without feeling threatened, and she could also join in playing to whatever part she wishes, with which ever participant she takes a fancy to. Although these are the two basic types of enquiries, there are of course lots of variations to these themes. I can quite honestly say that whilst I have been offering my services for nearly 9 years, I have never yet had two separate clients with the same requirements, very similar but never exactly the same. Which is good otherwise what a boring life it would be if every one were the same.

So there you have the basic reasons for the couples enquiries. Whether it makes sense to you the reader, I don't know, but you must keep an open mind and not judge others by your own standards, as I have said; it takes all kinds in this world and who the hell am I to judge.

Well after quite a few phone calls from one particular couple, an appointment was made but only after speaking with the female on her own, which incidentally is something I insist on. I have in the past found that a lot of the initial inquiries are made by the male off his own back, without the full knowledge of his partner. Then when they arrive she knows nothing of the full depth of the conversations that has gone on between him and myself, leaving her looking quite bewildered by the whole thing. I have found it is always best to clarify the situation with the lady of this trio before they arrive, just to be sure. This being done and I was satisfied that she was fully aware of the situation I set the scene for their arrival.

I opened the door and he walked in with her still left out in the car, I think that he wanted to be sure that I was suitable for their requirements as well as the location, this being done he duly went back to the car and fetched his wife. They both went into the drawing room and sat down, to say that they were nervous would be an understatement. When I offered them either a glass of wine or a coffee, their reply was so quiet that I had to ask them to repeat the answer. Most people are shy on the arrival for their first appointment but these were more so. I had better take this one slowly I thought, how wrong I was. They wanted to get straight down to it without having time for niceties and getting to know each other in greater depths. This took me a little by surprise, however I did get time to chat to the female on her own to find out exactly her part in all this and how far she wanted to go with it. You must bear in mind that she was a very beautiful girl in her mid twenties with a figure to die for, having had no children her breasts were very firm and not a single stretch mark in sight. She was also very easy to talk to on her own and not a bit shy in her requirements, on the contrary she was extremely open and broad minded, and although this was her husbands fetish she was not going to be left out at all.

The scenario was for me to take the husband upstairs, and get him dressed into the most sissy/frilly attire I could fit him into, along with make-up, wigs and shoes. He was thirtyish; a security guard with a physique to match and obviously worked out in the gym, so to transfer him to a wimp was no easy task. Then when that was achieved she was to come into the bedroom, order him to sit on a chair in front of the bed and say absolutely nothing, just to watch her and Susie make love and have fun as a lesbian couple. At no time was he allowed to touch either of us, or take part in any of the games we may play, and his only form of relief was whatever he may do to himself by means of masturbation. So up the stairs he went entered the bedroom and waited for me to command him to strip. I made him wear some hold up stockings, pink frilly French knickers, white bra with large padding, leopard print short dress and black shoes with 2-inch heels. I applied lots of heavy make-up with bright red lipstick, put on a bright blonde bob wig and finished off with lots of cheap perfume. He really did look ridiculous especially with tattooed arms, and a moustache, never the less that was the whole idea. I then told him to sit on the given chair and wait for his beautiful wife to join us. I called her up stairs, and upon entering the bedroom she stared at her wimpish husband and laughed at him to his face, upon which he lowered his head in shame and never spoke a word. It became obvious to both of us that he was really excited by the whole affair. She then slowly stripped off her own clothes to reveal her gorgeous figure, along with an even, all over sun tan, only leaving on her black stockings, and silver jewellery contrasting against her mid length jet black hair. She really did look very very sexy and acted accordingly. I lowered the lighting, put on some quiet background music and stared sexily into her eyes; we then caressed each other and kissed passionately.

During all of this foreplay her husband was moaning louder and louder obviously getting very excited by what he was witnessing. I started to kiss her beautifully formed body all over, and I could tell that she was really enjoying the whole new experience.

Her husband was so worked up by now that he stood up and approached her to stroke her legs. Her response was to tell him to be seated immediately and not to try and touch again, as he was not allowed to do so. He was too wimpish for her to bother with. I cringed thinking to myself Christ I hope he doesn't get funny about all of this, as he was a big bugger and if he wanted too he was capable of knocking seven colours of s--t out of me. Fortunately she had him well under control, and he did just as she said. With that reassurance I carried on with my lesbian act with his wife. At this point she then reciprocated by going down on her knees in front of her husband, raising my short mini skirt, pulling down my panties to reveal my very erect manhood. Up to this point it had been hidden by all my female garments. I don't wish to boast, but I wasn't at the back of the queue when penises where handed out [I wasn't at the front either] but lets say I'm better than average. As I am well shaved and smooth all over the sight of my proud manhood was a very pleasant surprise to her and she let it be known to her sissy husband that she was more than pleased with what I had to offer. To say that for what I was about to receive may I be truly thankful would be an understatement, for she then gave me some of the best oral I have ever had. Right in front of her wimpish husband, who by now with what he was witnessing, started to use a full array of four lettered words in-between his ever louder moaning. By now I really didn't give a toss about him or what he may do, I was on cloud nine and enjoying every thing she was doing to me.

After about 15 minutes I noticed that the husband had gone very quiet and by now I was the one doing all the moaning. I glanced toward him and saw that he had long finished his personal masturbation and was just staring at his beautiful wife with her eyes closed, enjoying herself to oblivion without a care for him in the world.

I think it was her way of telling him that you got me into this and now I am going to make the best of it, and if you don't like it well that's tough you should have thought of that before. Her enthusiasm knew no boundaries, as I was about to find out. She then slowly stood up in front of me, placed her arms around me kissed me passionately, then pulled me toward the waiting bed. Instead of lying down, she placed herself on all fours in front of me, turned her head to one side to face me smiled and said with a sultry voice "please". Well what can you do when put in that position, I mean after all they are paying for a service and I must ensure that they get full customer satisfaction. I duly obliged to the best of my ability.

It was at about this point that the husband wanted to put an end to this little game by calling her name and saying "that's enough now, I am satisfied". "Are you now" was her reply," well I am not fully convinced of that so sit down, shut up watch and learn". My reaction to this was if there is a God up there please protect me now, for this bloke could go berserk and bloody kill me now if he so wished. Thankfully he did exactly as he was told, and allowed us both to complete our lovemaking to a fulfilled completion. After we had both got our breath back, I calmly stood up showed them where the bathroom and shower was, gave them each a clean towel, and then left them alone to talk of their adventure and prepare themselves for there journey home.

I went back down the stairs and made us all a pot of tea [the English mans answer to everything] to refresh ourselves whilst reminiscing over the last two hours. I wanted to make sure that they were both happy with the service that I had provided. Although I had convinced myself that they wouldn't be coming back because of the fact that his wife and I had probably gone further than he originally intended. To my pleasant surprise they were both very happy with the events that had taken place, and said that they couldn't wait until the next time, and as soon as he had saved some more pennies they would be back.

True to their word they have paid me several visits since that eventful day.

Now you may not agree with their actions, or you may be envious, but whatever your opinion is, they are happy, and if that's what keeps them together and happy, who are you to disagree, as I have said many times it takes all sorts in this world.

Chapter 13
THE BOYFRIEND

The title sounds a little ominous, but let me assure you all now I don't class myself as gay or even bisexual, but I have learnt to come to terms with my gender identity by completely separating the two very different sides of me. That is to say that when I am a man in male mode that's exactly what I am, and if I were ever to be approached by another man whilst in this mode all hell would be let loose. For whilst being a man I am like every other hot blooded male and simply adore the female of the species, and as old as I am I still enjoy the challenge of charming a beautiful available woman. Taking them to some fancy restaurant for a wonderful romantic meal, where we can talk for hours whilst swooning in each other's eyes over late night liquors and coffee.

But on the other hand when I am in my female mode as Susie, I enjoy the company of males, and like to be treated as a woman. Listening to all of that bullshit that men give out to us women to try and impress us, [and as a man I am probably no different]. I also enjoy the power us women have over you men knowing that when we have you hooked, we can twist you around our little finger, watching you squirm. Trust me guys you think that you are the strongest of the species, but let me tell you in that race you come second, and that's how it will always be.

So with that being said I have learnt to separate the two sides of me very successfully and never the twain shall meet, apart from when I have to act as a lesbian [now that really does get complicated]. Even so by keeping the two separated helps me to accept my duo life and get on with each side of it to the full. So when Ian contacted me for an appointment with a difference I was intrigued to say the least.

The day set for his appointment soon came, and when I eventually opened the door on his arrival, was pleasantly surprised on his appearance. A very smart young good looking office manager, who was extremely nervous in my presence to the point of being shy. Well Susie being Susie soon got him calmed down enough to tell me of his intriguing fantasy which for a married man with a young daughter quite surprised me. He wasn't just after 2 hours of relaxing fun, but something more permanent, he wanted a secret girlfriend, a mistress, a bit on the side in other words.

From what I could make of it I think his job was very demanding with lots of pressure, his wife who also worked had a very similar job with the same demands, so as far as I could make out they were drifting apart, each in their own separate ways. Communication between them was limited to the occasional argument, and if it wasn't for the sake of the daughter they would separate, she is of a different religion to him, of which she takes quite seriously. She had also put on a lot of weight, and what is more had gone right off sex, through some internal female illness, honestly I feel like Marge Proops sometimes, talk about agony aunt I hear it all.

Thankfully I am a good listener and can very often offer some good advice [it must be the woman in me] although in this case I think he was beyond taking anything on board I may have said to find a solution. He was looking for someone to spend the occasional afternoon with where he could escape all of his problems, and fulfil all of his fantasies with. After spending an hour or so with Susie he decided that I met the criteria. Firstly I looked very convincing, very smart but also very sexy, by dressing to please a mans needs. I was also very opened minded with my roll play services, and most of all a very good and understanding listener. We then discussed his fantasies, which were all over the place, sometimes he wanted to be dominant, sometimes he wanted to be submissive, and sometimes he just wanted a boyfriend/girlfriend experience. This would entail occasional outings in his car to various places, ranging from a countryside drive, to a city shopping trip whenever he could find a feasible excuse to get time away from his wife. Normally I would never leave the safety of my own home, but with Ian I felt safe, the one thing that I have learnt in life's lessons is to have the ability to judge peoples integrity. I have not always been right, but in this case I was prepared to go with my judgement.

So I went along with his requests and said that I would be prepared to accept his offer, but to leave the outings until we had built up a bond of trust between us. I explained to him that I feel very vulnerable when out of my own environment dressed as a female, this he understood and agreed with my request. Actually he thought that as we are in the middle of summer with long light evenings it would be better to wait until the longer darker evenings are upon us to help build my own confidence up to a level where I felt more comfortable. Up to this point my only encounters of going out dressed were with my ex wife who gave me great support and always protected me when needed. Even then it was only usually to designated venues where transvestites go [clubs etc].

Ian's first appointment got off to a flyer, and when the talking was over I asked him what sort of scenario he would like today, as we still had plenty of time left before he had to report back to his wife for his evening meal which he informed me was served at 6.30 sharp. He had wangled an afternoon off away from the office; it seemed a pity to waste the remaining time left. "Oh" he said "I would love to be completely controlled by you as my domineering girlfriend who is having a bad day and needs someone to take it out on. As I am your adoring boyfriend who will do anything to please and make you happy, I will leave everything to you to decide on what you think is fitting". With that said he just sat staring at me with those puppy dog eyes.

"Well in that case I am going to go upstairs to my bedroom which is the second door on the left at the top of the landing. Give me a couple minutes, then come on up and pay me a surprise visit". His puppy eyes lit like two headlamps on a car." Ok" he said. So off I went, when reaching my room I popped on some appropriate music [girly stuff] and waited for him to arrive, whilst trying to think of some type of situation I could put us in to carry the game further. As I looked around my bedroom for some inspiration I saw an old holiday postcard sent to me years ago by an old friend BINGO, that's it. When Ian entered the room I sat there looking all worried, and his obvious reaction was to ask me what was the problem. "You wouldn't understand you are a man" I exclaimed with a sharp voice. "Try me" he said. "Well I have been invited on holiday with one of my girlfriends to one of those Spanish islands where the nightlife never ends and she has all the latest sexy fashioned clothes with a figure to match. Look at me all my clothes are frumpy, she will be the centre of attraction and I will be left out in the cold". "Oh no you wont" he said. "You have got a lovely figure, a pretty face, and a gorgeous pair of legs, you will be chased by all of those hot blooded Spaniards and I won't be there to keep them off you". "Well what about the clothes?" I asked, [acting like a proper girl wanting everything]. "Show me what you have in your wardrobe and I will tell you what looks great on you". To which I replied. " The problem with that is when I start to give you a fashion parade you will have your hands all over me and distract us from sorting out my clothes. Unless I can restrain you some way it wont work, yes that's what I will do tie your hands up then you wont be able to touch, better still I will suspend you. With that I lowered some equipment which is present in my playroom for those really submissive slaves that visit me, Ian's eyes nearly popped out of his head when he saw what was in store for him. By the time I had lowered the restraining bar from the ceiling by pulleys and chain his wrists were eagerly waiting for the leather straps that were attached to it. Once securely fitted I hoisted him up really tight so that he was standing on tip toe with arms stretched upwards to the limit, now I had him just where I wanted him, so let the teasing begin. With him staring at my every movement I slowly lowered my skirt to reveal my black lace top shiny stockings with matching suspenders and thong. Still wearing my black patent high heeled shoes I walked slowly around him making sure that I brushed against him whilst doing so, but completely ignoring him as I did so. Then with the music playing slightly louder I started to swing my hips to the rhythm of the beat but keeping my back to him at the same time. I pulled out of my wardrobe what can only be described as a belt, it's the shortest mini skirt I have in black leather, which I found out was Ian's favourite material. I then slipped off my shoes, went to the spare room and fetched my thigh length black leather boots, sat on the bed in front of him and slowly put them on, using his body to push against whilst zipping them up to my thighs. This had a devastating effect on poor old Ian, who started to writhe on his suspended arms. I then went back to the spare room and out of Ian's sight put on a black leather basque along with a black leather jacket, then walked back to show my devoted suspended boyfriend the leather chick look. Up until that point I did not realise that poor Ian stuttered when highly excited, but I soon found that out when I asked him for his opinion on my appearance in the nightclub look. He reminded me of Arkwright in open all hours, with his remark of "ffffffffu---ng hell it cccccertainly does it fffffffor me, ppppplease darling cccccccccan you please lllet me down my arms are rrrrrrrreally aching". " Ummm" I said trying to hide my laughter at his sudden speech impediment. "Yes I will then you can polish off all of the dust on my boots, better still I will get you the black shoe polish and you can really rub some cream into the leather to soften them back up, as they are supposed to be soft leather boots. As I released him from his restraints he fell straight to his knees to touch the boots and feel the softness for himself.

" Now you just stay there on your knees whilst I fetch the polish, cream, and cloths for your chores, and don't move until my return" I commanded. "Nnnnnno I wont" he again stuttered, When I returned some 3 minutes later I couldn't help but notice the very large bulge in the front of his trousers. As I sat on the bed in front of him and beckoned him to crawl towards me to fullfill his cleaning task mentioned that if he didn't soon remove his trousers the zip will split open and break. "Remove them now "I said with a stern voice, he didn't need telling that twice. He went back on his knees revealing his very stiff and erect penis, which was uncontrollably twitching and pulsing with excitement. " Now get to work and clean my boots then soften them with that special cream". I have never seen anyone work with such enthusiasm rubbing and polishing, then when he went to put on the cream he was shaking with excitement, so I let one of my boots gently touch his throbbing manhood, now he shook and stuttered all at the same time. "Jjjjjjjjjesus Mary mother of God, he screamed then with eyes tightly closed let out what can only be described as a cross between a loud moan and a scream, then as if he had passed out lay his head on my stocking topped thighs, closed his eyes once more and just let out a relieving sigh. What on earth is happening I thought, then when I looked down I could see exactly for myself what had happened, I think darling you had better clean that right boot again don't you? Yes you guessed it the right boot was a part white boot

I don't know when was the last time poor old Ian had sex with his wife, but I have never to this day seen a man so frustrated and worked up as he was. That was over two years ago now and Ian is still one of my favourites, we have had many a fun afternoon together, all with differing scenarios, but all with the same effect as the first one. He really has become my boyfriend and phones me on a regular basis just for a chat. It has been good for both of us, as we all need friends What is that they say?' a problem shared is a problem halved'. Very true, and I hope he can say the same for me, I only wish I could return his true friendship in a more open way, but with him standing by his marriage obligations it is very difficult. I do respect him for that. I just hope that one day the two of them get their act together and find the happiness they deserve with each other, I am sure they will eventually. I will know when that happens, as the lovely parcelled presents, and letters will no doubt stop arriving at my door, along with the frequent bunches of flowers.

The one footnote I should add to Ian's problems, it is the fact that he has brought a lot of them on his self. He has been a transvestite admirer for many years, long before he even got married, and I am just one of many others to whom he has paid attention, so knowing that fact he should have questioned his conscience before getting married.

Chapter 14
TAKING THE PISS

This client is one of a rare breed in his requirements, not so much in the fact that he is a very submissive man who occupies a high-flying job. In his case he is in a professional position, which is quite common. I have found that in almost all cases of people, who have a strong need to be dominated, they themselves are in a position of power in their career. Especially where the law is concerned [I will say no more but leave you to draw your own conclusions]. As I have said before there are no two scenarios the same, as there is no two people the same, similar but not the same, so back to my rare client, he is into water sports, golden shower, or as the chapter states, taking the piss.

One of the strangest things about this client is the fact he was well known to me long before he became a client, in fact he has done a lot of work for my development company in his professional capacity. So imagine the shock to me when he answered my advert in the weekly rag. Of course as I have a separate phone for my escorting work with its own number he would not have had a clue that it was me he was going to be talking to over the phone. That was where I had an advantage over him, as I knew his number. You would have thought that he would have had the sense to use a different phone for his private fetishes but no not him. Fortunately for me when I answer the phone in my female mode I always disguise my voice in a more feminine way, so he didn't even recognise me when talking to me for the first time in reply to the advert. But how on earth was I going to bring to his attention just who I really am, especially after he had opened up on the phone telling me all of his strange requests. Then out of the blue by sheer coincidence I received an invoice from him for work done for my company, and I thought bugger it if he is going to charge me that much for that piddling amount of work he has done for me then its about time I got some of it back. He was phoning me on a regular basis for an appointment with Susie, up to this point I had failed to give him a firm date, purely to avoid his embarrassment, leaving him repeatedly pestering me for a visit. So my plan of attack was as Peter, to ask him to come to my office to discuss his latest invoice, then when he arrived I would be dressed as Susie and spill the beans. Better to do it to his face, rather than over the phone, after all he had already told me all about his private side of life, so it was me who was going to feel embarrassed when he was to find out the truth. At the end of the day what can he do, I know just as much about his seedy fetishes as he will of mine, in other words he will have as much to loose as me, more in fact. You can imagine the shocked look on his face when I opened the door for his so-called visit to Peter for some money. "Come in darling" I calmly, said and with mouth still opened wide he did just that. You could see the sheer look of amazement on his face, and as he sat in my office I revealed to him just who I was, well this is Susie, we have already chatted a lot on the phone, remember? As the penny was slowly dropping his open mouth changed to a pleasant smile, good god he said I would never have guessed in a million years, I really cant believe its you, the difference is phenomenal. You look so attractive, and convincing, gorgeous in fact, the transformation is absolutely amazing. Well that's one hurdle out of the way I thought, now for the next one. "Well now that you can see me for what I am and know that you have told me all about yourself, would you still like to visit me as Susie and fulfil your fantasies with me?" "Even more so" came his reply; with by now a larger smile on his face, "Well in that case we had better discuss this invoice of yours and how it can be paid, any suggestions?" Knowing full well that no cash would be changing hands came his reply. "Well what about if you can work off your bill with me as Susie, you know let me visit you and every time I do we will call that a part payment". Being a businessman I said, "ok but I will need some discount". "How much?" he asked. "Ten percent" I said " well if I was going to pay you cash today in full I would ask for the same, so what is the difference?" He nodded in agreement.

So an appointment was made there and then for his first visit, and we spent the rest of his appointed time that day discussing his requirements in great depth. Its funny but looking at him whilst he opened up all of his fetishes to me, revealing that he was a long time transvestite admirer, really astounded me for I would never have thought that he was that kind of person. I must admit I looked upon him in a different way from that day onwards, not necessarily in a bad way for who am I to judge, just different. He informed me that he likes to be stripped naked, tied up, with a dog collar around his neck and worship my body, my feet in particular. Especially licking my shoes as well as my feet, then severely thrashed on his bare buttocks with a riding crop so many on each cheek, making sure that he was well and truly marked. He then wanted to be urinated on all over whilst on his knees before me, also making sure that I did the same in his mouth making sure that he had to swallow some of it. To do this I was to place a clamp over his nose ensuring that he had to keep his mouth open to breath, and finally he wanted to have his nipples tortured, by means of clamping, piercing, pinching, and twisted. Not all at the same time I said, that's far too much pain in one go, its best to split it up and take it one stage at a time. " Well if you say so mistress I will leave it all up to you to administer as you see fit". I had to explain to him that there was a lot of preparation to do with various props for each of the differing types of scenarios.

For instance when I do water sports I have a large four-foot square plastic tray with a 4inch-upsturned apron, which is placed, on the bedroom/playroom floor. You have stand or kneel whatever the case, to perform this act; otherwise it will go all over the floor. Then for the tying up there are restraints and various leg spreaders including chains and pulleys, that have to be fixed and secured to the ceiling then lowered accordingly. All of this he understood and agreed with me that we would do a different scenario each time to allow full and proper use of all of the equipment. What he would do was to phone me a day before each appointment and tell me what type of scenario he wanted so that I could prepare accordingly in plenty of time. I mean imagine fixing all of that equipment up too soon when someone wanted an appointment and they saw all of that stuff. If they were of the nervous variety wanting a mild domination scenario, it would frighten the living daylights out of them, so you can see its not as simple as you may think, there is an awful lot of preparation and clearing up afterwards to do.

Well true to his word the day before his appointment he, as promised phoned me to express his wishes for the following days role-play. It was at this point that I started to doubt his ability to be able to accept all of what he had been asking for. In the past I have found that a lot of the sexual thrill is in the head, and when it comes to reality it does not have the desired effect they thought it would have. In other words pain overtakes any thrill they may be getting. He was asking for a really good hard thrashing with the riding crop [which incidentally does bloody hurt] whilst tied face down on the bed and secured to the bed itself, gagged to muffle the sound of his screams. It all sounded a bit too much to me especially for the first time. What made me suspicious was the way in which he was telling me, it was like a kid at Christmas, very excited, talking 20 to the dozen, his head was well and truly away with the fairies, and not thinking of the consequences in reality terms.

So the next day when he eventually arrived I made him strip naked before me in the hallway, then placing a dog collar around his neck with an attached lead, pulled him up the stairs behind me like a scolded dog. By the time we had reached the top of the stairs the first complaint came out." The collar is too tight mistress" "tough" I replied "that's nothing you wait until I thrash you then you will have something to complain about!" I then pulled him through the bedroom door, turned to face him and ordered him to worship his mistress by going down on his knees and worshipping her feet and licking her shoes especially the heels. This he did without question, then the next complaint "my knees are hurting mistress" "keep quiet you wimp" I scowled. " I will tell you when you can get up, until then you stay there and worship me". I now knew that my suspicions were not unfounded but just to be sure I will see how he takes to the riding crop. "Get up slave" I shouted, "then lay your worthless body on the bed face down and prepare yourself for my pleasure in giving you some pain". Talk about all in the head I kid you not. After securing him to the bed and tying his hands and feet together making sure that the ropes were not too tight for him to moan about, I started to swish the crop in the air just to make it sound effective, well he started to yell. " Please not too hard mistress, I must not be marked in case my wife sees them". What a turn around I thought I haven't even touched him yet, and no sooner than I placed the first very gentle stroke against his bare buttock he was screaming out the pre arranged safety word; orange. Which means stop I don't like it, now not wishing to pay his bill with cash I stopped. "What's the matter?" I asked." I think it would be nice for you to start very gently just to warm me up, then get a little harder", he said. "That's what I was doing" I told him. "Well it really does hurt mistress", "it is supposed to that's what you asked for!" I exclaimed. "Well can you not use the crop try your hand gently first just to get me used to it then try the crop". As soon as my hand slapped his arse off he screamed out again " orange".

I could see it was pointless to continue and suggested that he get dressed and come back down stairs where we could have another talk about his requirements. When we finally sat down in the living room he then told me that he has never before done the things he asked me for, but that the thought of having them done really turned him on. "You should have told me that before", I said. "Then I would have explained to you that it was all in your head and that when it comes to having the real thing it is not as good as you first think. To be a complete submissive slave able to take your mistresses punishment takes time and patience in the build up and conversion from pain to pleasure". He had no option but to agree.

Thankfully he was not put off by that first experience, and was soon back to experiment further this time with the water sports. Now there was no problem with this, in fact he took to that like a duck to water [pardon the pun]. In fact he revels in it, just as well because for two hours or so before he arrives I have to drink glasses and glasses of water to make sure I have a full bladder for my devoted slave.

He even drinks some of it out of a glass which he will obediently hold before me whilst on his knees, then wait for my command to swallow. He has even been known on occasions when I have been seeing another client and he was perhaps in the area, to enter my home whilst I have been upstairs entertaining and drink my urine out of a glass which I have left full for him in my downstairs cloakroom all pre arranged of course. Whilst the present client upstairs with me knew nothing of what was happening in the cloakroom.

As for the rest of his fantasies, I have now brought him on in leaps and bounds; he can take the riding crop at least 30 strokes on each cheek, with full marks. His nipples also get the preferential treatment, with fierce clamps, well pinched and stretched at the same time, lots of hot candle wax every where, and of course lots and lots of body/foot worship. He never ever complains about the ropes or collar being too tight, all in all he has taken his training schedule very very well, and become one of my well-behaved slaves, giving 100% satisfaction to his strict mistress. Mind you it has taken at least 25 visits to get him to this point, but in fairness to him he is more enthusiastic now than he has ever been. It is not just one phone call I get before his visits but several going over and over again all what he wants on his next appointment. [I must check my bill it must be paid in full by now].

Chapter 15
TWIST IN THE TALE

Its funny but for nearly all of my life I have been ashamed in one way or another of my feminine side. Although Susie has never been anything than proud of Peter the same cannot be said for the reverse. In times past when the chips have been down Peter has always kept Susie in the cupboard safely locked away until circumstances started to look up a little then only letting her out in small doses.

Yet when my last marriage broke up and the chips were really down, both in my personal loneliness living in a large 4-bedroom house with all its memories and in my business. My wife's departure coincided with one of the worst financial crashes in recent history leaving me to battle on to complete my final contract including doing all the donkey work. It's fair to say that the situation was once again at rock bottom.

There is no doubt about it that given the same circumstances in times gone by Peter would have most certainly put Susie straight into the cupboard and probably thrown away the key. The one thing I do have to thank my ex wife for is the fact that she helped me to come to terms with my split life and accept Susie for who she is and not to be ashamed of her or her ways. In those early weeks of single loneliness and all round pressure for the first time ever in my life as Peter I leaned on Susie for support and surprisingly found it.

Not only did Susie help Peter in a financial way but also in a supporting role. She gave Peter the strength to face up to all of those problems life seems to throw at you. Believe me its true when they say "a problem shared is a problem halved" and like a giant snowball rolling down the hill seemed to overcome my moments of weakness and gained strength in my present situation with lots of help from Susie.

This really was a new twist in my life as now in my early sixties I was not only accepting Susie but also using her for strength and when in dressed as Susie all of Peters troubles vanished.

Whilst all of this was going on my son who is approaching 40 was concerned of my well being given all of the traumatic happenings going on in my life. As he lives some 150 miles away he offered to come and stay with me for a short period to give me some support and company. Knowing of my previous illnesses he must have thought to himself that he had better go and check on the old man in case he pops his clogs and get his name on the will as soon as possible.

He knows all about Susie and is fully supportive of her existence. No one laughs more than he does when I relay some of Susie's experiences.

Being a practical man as I am I have never been one to get into computers although I do have one in my office and have had for nearly three years. I did not have a clue of even how to switch one on and in the past used to wait until the school bus stopped outside my house in the afternoon for my neighbour's fourteen-year-old son. I would pay him a couple of quid to sit behind my desk and operate this electrical gadget typing emails, letters and so on enabling me to be seen to be operating in the twenty first century. Word soon got around down my street that I was some sort of retard with more money than sense.

So my son in his wisdom thought it about time I learnt to operate one of these things for my self saying "Dad there is a whole new world out there and once you have learnt to use one it will open all sorts of new doors for you." Well how right he was, what is it they say 'out of the mouths of babes'. Like I have said before "you are never too old to learn". To my pride as Peter and sometimes Susie I have even managed to write this book on one. My typing skills have surprised me [thank God for spellchecker].

My son even taught me how to look up sites on the net that cater for transvestites and how useful they can be!

So I joined up to one particular site and that in itself has been one of the best things that has happened to me. I found a whole new world of like minded people right on my doorstep which has resulted in me forming some really good friendships .One in particular a tv called Jenny has become a really good friend with lots of common interests. Between us we have formed our own group of likeminded tvs who meet up once a month at my house for social gatherings and frequent parties.

These parties caused a bit of a stir with some of my neighbours.... Only because they felt left out, as they had often attended parties thrown by my wife and I. Having already come out to one neighbour who had suspected Peters other side she told me of the gossip. Taking the bull by the horns I went to see my close neighbours and told them all expecting them to be horrified and never wishing to talk to me again. To my surprise they were extremely supportive saying "you will always be Peter to us" and in fact asked if they could come to our next party. They did and attend regularly now always enjoying themselves with their eyes and mouths wide open.

As a result of these meetings I along with Jenny have made lots of new friends including some supportive wives who between them have encouraged Susie to venture out into the wider world of nightclubs and tv friendly bars. This was a big step forward for Susie having only ever gone out before with my ex-wife to pre-selected venues so to meet the general public face on was a huge step for Susie. To be fair to my friends we always go out in groups of at least 3. With the other 2 in the group being used to going out this has helped e to overcome my fear of meeting the general public no end.

On our very first outing to a cosmopolitan city upon entering a bar for the first time as Susie was confronted by a large group of Scotsmen all in kilts. They were in town for a sporting event and had just seen their team lose and so were drowning their sorrows and were by now slightly worse for wear. To say the atmosphere was heavy would be an understatement.

As we stood at the bar alone in a room full of jocks getting a little bit rowdy I could see that my two friends were getting a little anxious of the situation, especially as we seemed to be the topic of their conversation. The fact that they stood between the door and us didn't help.

With that one of these Scottish gentlemen came up to the bar to order a fresh round of drinks as he stood right alongside of me you could hear a pin drop. With all of his fellow country men looking on I don't know to this day what came over me but I just felt that I had to say or do something. I just stood back a little looked him up and down then said to him "darling if you are going to wear a skirt like us you must shave your legs". At this point I noticed a look of horror on my friends faces but fortunately for us he took it in good heart. This really broke the ice and we spent the rest of our time in that bar in their company. Even taking one of their wives on to a nightclub with us later in the evening. She was absolutely fascinated by our appearance.

Jenny and I have both made a good friendship with another tv called Cheryl who is a part time singer. Like myself Jenny has also been a semi-professional musician in the past so the three of us decided to form a new trio of musicians with a difference. Yes you guessed it in femme mode with the three of us stood in a line each with her own mike singing to backing tracks of appropriate songs such as 'Pretty Woman'. Lets hope we don't get caught out under the Trades Description Act.

We call ourselves 'The Tranzsisters' and have our very first gig coming up very soon so watch out we could be in a town near you.

Looking back I can't help but think what a difference twelve months can make.

CONCLUDING THOUGHTS

Looking back at the broader picture of my life and its strange journeys, I don't think that I regret any part of it enough to want to change it. If I were to have that chance, I would of course love to alter the date of my fathers' death, to still have him here now. To be able to talk to and seek his advice. Even though I am approaching 63 you are never too old to listen to someone wiser. Mind you with me turning out as I have he may not want to know me, although I doubt that. Times have changed so much over the last 50 years, and like it or not we have all seemed to adapt to the modern ways, even the mightiest of oak trees will bend in the wind.

As for the clients that I have mentioned in my book, I have of course given all of them different names and professions to protect them, and I will never ever reveal their true identity under any circumstances. They are just a small minority of my clientele and there are many more with just as varying sexual fantasies as the ones already mentioned. I suppose that if I had to break down the statistics I would say that 70% like domination of some form or another 20% like the boyfriend/girlfriend experience and 10% are just curious to try anything.

But on the whole I really do enjoy most of my clients and their fantasies and they tell me that it shows in my performances. Which is just as well because like every one else I need to keep the Wolf from the door. How long I will be able to continue with my present chosen profession is another question, the one thing to remember is that as I am getting older, so are they.

I hope that you have enjoyed reading my life's story as much as I have enjoyed writing it, and if ever any of you are thinking about writing a book, then do so, because it has been one of the most therapeutic experiences I have ever encountered.

Whether this book is a success or not I have benefited so much personal satisfaction in just the writing of this book.

Good health and good luck to all of you.

Peter Edwards